TO:

———————————————

FROM:

———————————————

DATE:

———————————————

DEMI LEIGH TEBOW

KNOWING WHO YOU ARE BECAUSE OF WHO GOD IS

100 DAYS TO UNBREAKABLE FAITH

Knowing Who You Are Because of Who God Is
© 2025 Demi-Leigh Tebow

All rights reserved. No portion of this book may be reproduced, stored in a retrieval system, or transmitted in any form or by any means—electronic, mechanical, photocopy, recording, scanning, or other—except for brief quotations in critical reviews or articles, without the prior written permission of the publisher.

Published in Nashville, Tennessee, by Thomas Nelson. Thomas Nelson is a registered trademark of HarperCollins Christian Publishing, Inc.

Thomas Nelson titles may be purchased in bulk for educational, business, fundraising, or sales promotional use. For information, please email SpecialMarkets@ThomasNelson.com.

Unless otherwise noted, Scripture quotations are from the (NASB®) New American Standard Bible®. Copyright © 1960, 1971, 1977, 1995, 2020 by The Lockman Foundation. Used by permission. All rights reserved. www.lockman.org.

Scripture quotations marked CSB are from the Christian Standard Bible®. Copyright © 2017 by Holman Bible Publishers. Used by permission. Christian Standard Bible® and CSB® are federally registered trademarks of Holman Bible Publishers.

Scripture quotations marked ESV are from the ESV® Bible (The Holy Bible, English Standard Version®). Copyright © 2001 by Crossway, a publishing ministry of Good News Publishers. All rights reserved.

Scripture quotations marked NASB1995 are from the New American Standard Bible®. Copyright © 1960, 1971, 1977, 1995 by The Lockman Foundation. Used by permission. All rights reserved. www.lockman.org.

Scripture quotations marked NIV are from the Holy Bible, New International Version®, NIV®. Copyright © 1973, 1978, 1984, 2011 by Biblica, Inc.® Used by permission of Zondervan. All rights reserved worldwide. www.zondervan.com. The "NIV" and "New International Version" are trademarks registered in the United States Patent and Trademark Office by Biblica, Inc.

Scripture quotations marked NLT are from the Holy Bible, New Living Translation. Copyright © 1996, 2004, 2015 by Tyndale House Foundation. Used by permission of Tyndale House Publishers, Carol Stream, Illinois 60188. All rights reserved.

Scriptures marked NET are from the NET Bible®. http://netbible.com. Copyright © 1996, 2019 by Biblical Studies Press, L.L.C. Used by permission. All rights reserved.

Any internet addresses, phone numbers, or company or product information printed in this book are offered as a resource and are not intended in any way to be or to imply an endorsement by Thomas Nelson, nor does Thomas Nelson vouch for the existence, content, or services of these sites, phone numbers, companies, or products beyond the life of this book.

Cover design and photography by Micah Kandros.
Illustrations by Jolindi van der Merwe.

ISBN 978-1-4002-5074-5 (hardcover)
ISBN 978-1-4002-5076-9 (audiobook)
ISBN 978-1-4002-5075-2 (eBook)

Printed in Malaysia
25 26 27 28 29 TOM 10 9 8 7 6 5 4 3 2 1

To my daughter—
Before you ever take your first breath,
you are known. Before you speak
your first word, you are loved.

If you ever find yourself questioning your
worth, value, or identity: May you look
to who God is, and may that always be a
reflection and a reminder of who you are.

You are fearfully and wonderfully
made, created with purpose to rule
and to reign. Walk in His truth, rest
in His grace, and never forget: You
are His, and that is enough.

With all my love,
Mama

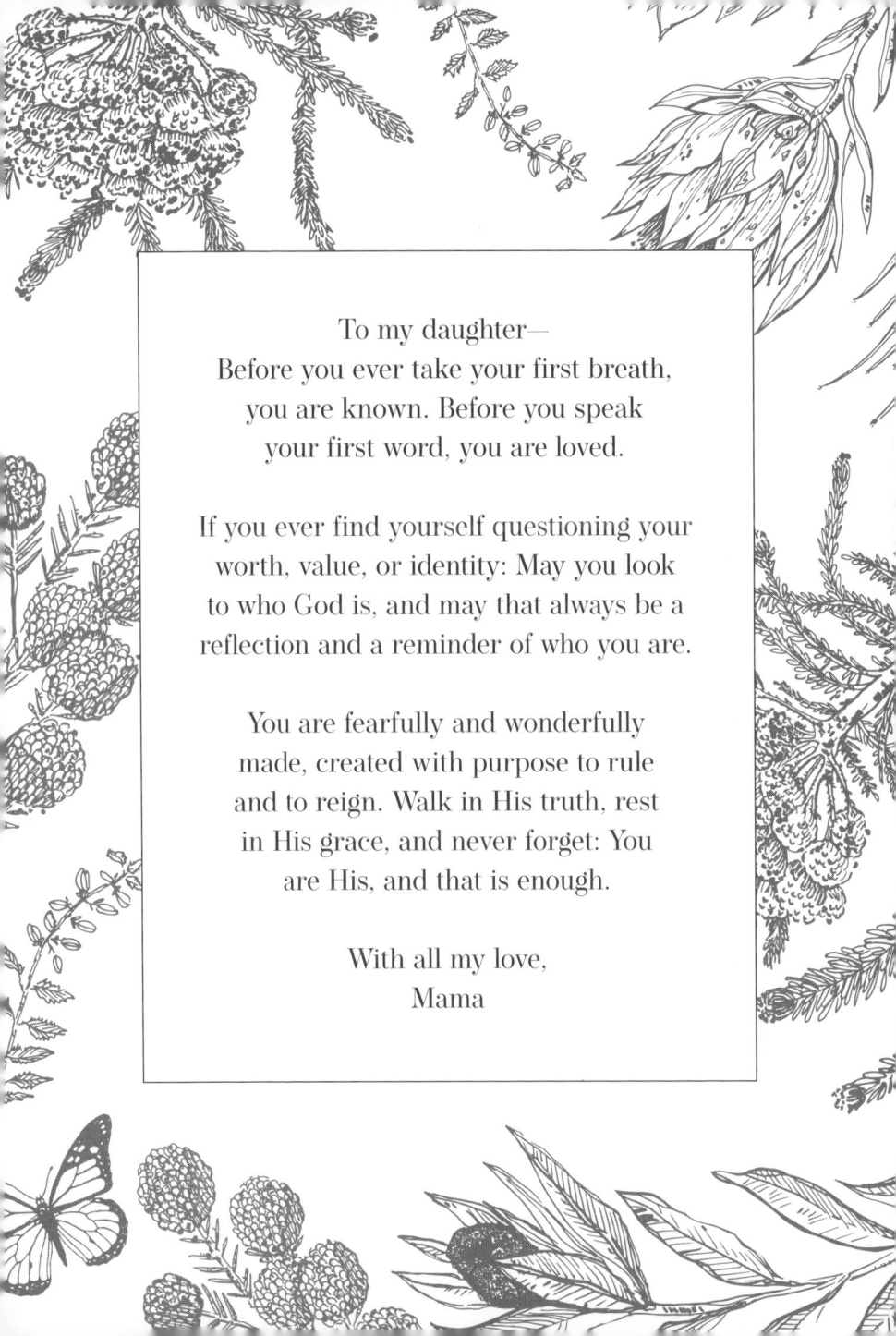

Contents

A Note from Demi vii

KNOWING WHO YOU ARE

Week 1   You are not your label. 3

Week 2   You belong with God. 13

Week 3   You are precious to God. 23

Week 4   You have been forgiven. 33

Week 5   You can wait because God is worth it. 43

Week 6   You have no room for shame. 53

Week 7   You have access to endless wisdom. 63

Week 8   You may be weak, but Christ 73

Week 9   You are invited to carry out God's purpose. 83

Week 10   You can have peace, no matter your circumstance. . . 93

BECAUSE OF WHO GOD IS

Week 11 God's love for you is unbreakable and inseparable. . . 107

Week 12 God offers you the greatest gift in the world through Jesus. 117

Week 13 God is good. Always. 127

Week 14 God is always with you. 137

Week 15 God is the ultimate helper. 147

Week 16 God's Word offers soul satisfaction. 157

Week 17 God's ways and thoughts are higher than yours. . . . 167

Week 18 God is forever faithful. 177

Week 19 God will finish what He started in you. 187

Week 20 God is a promise keeper. 197

Final Thoughts 208
Acknowledgments 209
Notes 210
About the Author 213

A NOTE FROM DEMI

Has anyone ever offered you clichéd advice? You know, something like:

Fake it till you make it.
Follow your heart.
Keep going—you've got this, girl!

Or maybe someone made you a promise that wasn't theirs to make and you believed it—something like:

Everything you need to succeed is already inside of you.
It's all going to be okay.
If you believe in yourself, you can do anything.

These lines might sound nice in the moment or work in the short term, but they aren't rooted in biblical truths. Relying on false beliefs or striving to be a new or better version of yourself won't give you lasting confidence. Rather, knowing how God sees you will produce a confidence that doesn't come from superficial assurance but from promises rooted in a faithful God.

Over the next one hundred days, we'll explore age-old promises from God that still hold true today. Each weekly promise is divided into five daily readings—labeled Plot, Dig, Plant, Grow, and Flourish—with practical information for you to apply in your own life. In my book *A Crown That Lasts*, I share my faith journey through plant imagery—with the concepts of digging, planting, growing, and flourishing. In this devotional, which is meant to guide you to a more confident, unbreakable faith, we'll plot our course for the week, then dig, plant, grow, and flourish together as we consider promises about who we are because of who God is.

You may be thinking, *Demi, there are more than five days in a week!* You're right—but the goal of this devotional is to be a blessing in your life, not a burden. You can use this devotional over the course of one hundred consecutive days, or you can walk with me through twenty five-day weeks. I want to offer you this option because everyone is busy, and life can escape us quickly. I encourage you to use the remaining two days each week to catch up on what you've missed, practice what we've been discussing, or spend time with your church community, building fellowship and worshiping together.

With that said, let's talk about our goals for each week.

Plot: It's essential to survey the land and decide where you'd like to dig before planting new greenery. And that's precisely what we will do on the first day of each week. We'll take time to set our heart posture by getting acquainted with the promise of the week and truthfully evaluating what areas of our life require new seeds of truth to be planted.

Dig: Day 2 will require some blood, sweat, and tears. Okay, maybe I'm exaggerating, but this is a day of putting in some hard work! Transparency and perhaps a little vulnerability about how you truly see yourself and the world around you will be key attributes of this day.

Plant: Now that we've dug up potential lies and seeds of doubt that have burrowed into our lives, day 3 is our time to plant new truths. We will discuss who we are and who God is based on our chosen verse for the week.

Grow: Good things come with time! Day 4 will focus on nourishing and cultivating the truths we planted on day 3. We will fill ourselves with God's Word and rest in the rays of His Spirit.

Flourish: Action is the difference between knowledge and belief. Day 5 is an encouragement to remember that week's promise by memorizing it and creating personal challenges that move knowledge toward action.

There are no tricks for living out God's purpose in your life. True strength and confidence come from knowing who you are in Christ and trusting in His plan for your life.

Are you ready? Let's grow!

Demi
xOxO

KNOWING
WHO
YOU ARE

WEEK NO. 1

Promise for Your Week:

YOU ARE NOT YOUR LABEL.

But you are a chosen race, a royal priesthood, a holy nation, a people for his own possession, that you may proclaim the excellencies of him who called you out of darkness into his marvelous light.

1 PETER 2:9 (ESV)

DAY 1

PLOT

Steve Harvey's voice echoed over the thunderous cheers and applause: "Take your first walk as Miss Universe!" Miss Philippines faced the ecstatic audience and walked into her new chapter as I turned the other way. My reign as Miss Universe had officially ended. My multifaceted support team—security guard, stylist, manager, videographer, and social media manager—all rushed past me to attend the new Miss Universe. Suddenly, I had become part of the scenery.

That night, I left far more than the Miss Universe crown on stage. I left behind an identity I had tied to that crown—an illusion of confidence born from achieving a lifelong dream. As my reign ended, it felt like the rug was being pulled out from under my six-inch heels. The change was so sudden, it left me wobbling as I attempted to find a new sense of stability.

Have you ever faced uncertainty after thinking you had everything figured out—a stable income, the perfect partner, the Instagram-worthy vacation? And then a cut, a call, or someone's actions forced you to reassess your path? Maybe a relationship ended, but your identity was tied to being a girlfriend, fiancée, or wife. Maybe an ordinary week was upended by a call from the doctor's office.

It's easy to label ourselves based on our circumstances, desires, or what others say about us. This week we'll focus on identifying some of these labels that we have allowed ourselves to be defined by. Then we'll look to God for a firm, eternal identity that gives true meaning and purpose!

PRAYER FOR YOUR DAY

Dear Lord, thank You for creating me and placing me where I am today. Help my eyes to be opened this week to the labels put on me by myself and others. Remind me this week how I am seen through Your eyes. Search me and know me, and let me see the lies I have believed so that I may rest in Your truth. In Jesus' name I pray, amen.

> **YOU ARE NOT YOUR LABEL.**

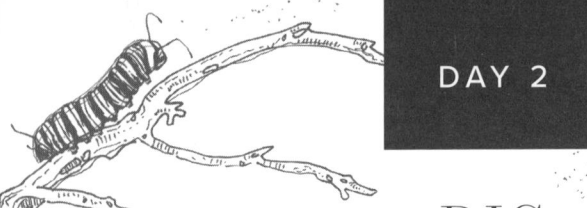

DAY 2

DIG

Identity can mean a lot of things, but it is primarily about how we see ourselves as a person. Oftentimes our life circumstances shape us into who we are. This includes accolades, titles, promotions, and relationships. While many of these are beautiful things that make life feel full and special, they can also become idols that keep us from fully trusting God.

Do you find your identity in any of these places? The problem with rooting our identity in our circumstances and relationships is that they are ever-changing, leading to a roller coaster of emotions influenced by low self-esteem, unanswered questions, and insecurities. An estimated 85 percent of people have experienced low self-esteem at some point in their lives.[1] It's no surprise that we struggle when we tie ourselves so strongly to things that can change.

I've learned that if I want lasting confidence in my identity, I'm going to have to root it in something *bigger than myself*, something *fixed*, *never changing*, and *always trustworthy*. What are you rooting your identity in? Is it something that meets those characteristics?

Does anything or anyone come to mind?

As much as I loved my Miss Universe crown and label, it was part of a temporary life circumstance. When it got stripped away, I was left grappling with an identity crisis. Maybe you've been there too. Who are you when the business you've built fails? When the career you've devoted decades to ends unexpectedly? When your most familiar role—as mother, daughter, friend—disappears? What do you do when your daily purpose vanishes? Losing my title caused me to realize how much of my worth I had tied to it. You might not have been a pageant queen, but we all have roles or achievements we value deeply. We all have labels we attach to ourselves.

What are the positive or negative labels you have placed on yourself or others have placed on you?

_____

_____

How comfortable are you wearing those labels? What if they were to change overnight or you had to give them up?

_____

_____

Are any of those labels clearly false or flimsy when you consider how God looks at you?

_____

_____

PRAYER FOR YOUR DAY

Lord, thank You for establishing my worth and value long before I was born. Allow me to identify the false or fleeting labels this world places on me and look to You for the truth. In Jesus' name, amen.

YOU ARE NOT YOUR LABEL.

DAY 3

PLANT

Now that we've identified some of the labels that have gotten stuck to us, whether we like them or not, let's explore how to peel those labels off, one by one, without allowing any residue to remain.

Understand who God created you to be. We weren't meant to be chasing after false praise, shallow security, or selfish pursuits. We were made for much more. Ephesians 2:10 says, "We are His workmanship, created in Christ Jesus for good works, which God prepared beforehand so that we would walk in them." God created us for *His* purposes, not our own. He invites us to participate with Him in what He's doing in our communities and the world. I've heard it said, "To love God is to serve God, and to serve God is to serve others." Our life's greatest goal should be a relationship with the One who created us. To be loved and fully known by Him. In turn, He will use our gifts, talents, experiences, and even our messy imperfections to point others to Him as we serve and love others along the way.

Identify how God made you perfectly unique. I used to believe that my life purpose should be connected to something rare or unconventional to be valuable. However, 1 Peter 2:9 reminds us that we are part of something incredibly special—"A chosen race, a royal priesthood, a holy nation, a people for [God's] own possession" (ESV). Therefore, our identity is not dependent on our earthly accolades but on the unique gifts and talents God has given each of us. I believe that our life's purpose and calling are often directly related to things we enjoy, appreciate, resonate with, and are naturally good at. Just as we are called "out of darkness into his marvelous light," we can use our specific abilities to glorify God.

When you peel off the false and fickle labels, you'll be able to put on the identity that He desires for you to embrace. You are God's workmanship, and you are uniquely called to His purpose. God has created you to do life with Him. He has blessed you with incredible talents to bring love, hope, and truth to others wherever you are. Be confident in what God can accomplish when you welcome His plan.

A PRAYER FOR YOU FROM ME

Dear Lord, thank You for the perfect purpose You have called this reader to. I ask that You give her the tools to peel off the labels she's been burdened with and give her the clarity not only to see but to walk in Your perfect plan. In Jesus' name, amen.

> **YOU ARE NOT YOUR LABEL.**

DAY 4

GROW

Even when we know our God-given identity and our unique purpose, that confidence will be tested again and again throughout our lives. One of the ways I've fallen prey to self-doubt is through the pressures and expectations of other people. Even years after handing over my Miss Universe title, I've had moments when a comment or statement made me completely doubt myself. I've even let comments from complete strangers affect me.

One of those moments happened shortly after I got married, when I accompanied my husband, Tim, to a speaking engagement. Backstage, one of the sweet older ladies in the meet-and-greet line asked me, "Now what? Do you have any hobbies? How are you going to keep yourself busy on the road, seeing that you married such a busy man?" This lady didn't know me at all and likely didn't mean to hit a sore spot, but without her realizing it, she had slapped a great big label on my forehead that read "Tim Tebow's Wife."

Her words made me question myself and my role as a new wife. Was I so easy to sum up as one thing? Was this my new, all-encompassing label? It made me wonder if pursuing my own dreams was the right thing to do now that I was married. Anxious thoughts rushed through my mind as I tried to process this stranger's comment.

It's usually in vulnerable moments like this when our self-confidence is shaken the most. I was new at the whole wife thing and needed to remind myself what my identity was, with or without my new last name. Besides, that was the person Tim ultimately fell in love with and decided to marry. But navigating a new identity takes time. Whether we've gained a new career or a new title, we're not always sure who we are in light of this change, leaving us vulnerable to external expectations.

Two of my life's greatest blessings are having found my life partner and getting to cheer him on every day. At that moment of self-doubt with this stranger, I realized that shifting my confidence and identity from my Miss Universe crown to my marriage wasn't going to give me everlasting purpose. Sure, shifting our roles from being a wife to a mom or from that corner office to that retirement package are all great things! However, no *one* identity is our *full* identity, and if we try to make it so, we don't leave room for our ultimate identity as God's beloved. The only label that truly matters is our God-given label, which tells us:

We are His royalty. (Romans 8:17)
We are His *masterpiece* in Christ. (Ephesians 2:10 NLT)
We are the *crown* of creation. (Psalm 8:5)
We are *wonderfully* and *fearfully* made, crafted with care and intention. (Psalm 139:14 NIV)

PRAYER FOR YOUR DAY

Heavenly Father, thank You for naming me Your daughter and giving me an eternal identity! In moments when the Enemy tries to blur my vision and make me rely on myself, remind me that I can instead rely on You. No earthly label will ever hold up to the eternal label of worth and value forever placed on me by You. Amen.

YOU ARE NOT YOUR LABEL.

DAY 5

FLOURISH

Today let's read, meditate on, and memorize 1 Peter 2:9.

On day 2, we exposed the labels we've carried in the past. Let's swap those flimsy labels for lasting ones! God is given many labels in the Bible. Read through these verses before answering the next question: Exodus 15:11–13; 34:6–7; Psalms 27:1; 54:4; 86:15; Luke 6:35; Romans 5:8.

After meditating on the verses above, what labels would you give God?

Now, with God's power and love fresh in our minds, let's turn the attention to ourselves. Read through the following verses about how God sees us: Psalm 8:4–5, 139:14; Romans 5:8; 8:17; Ephesians 2:10; 2 Corinthians 5:17.

What label does God give you as His creation?

If the 2 Corinthians 5:17 label is true about you, how would that affect how you interact with other people?

As a treasured daughter of the King, your trust and confidence in your God-given identity could help someone else find theirs!

A PRAYER FOR YOU FROM ME

Dear Lord, thank You for caring about the little details of our lives and calling us to a greater purpose beyond what the world sees in us. Do something new in this reader's life! Bless her as she walks with the label You give her and shares that beauty with the world. In Jesus' name, amen.

YOU ARE NOT YOUR LABEL.

WEEK NO. 2

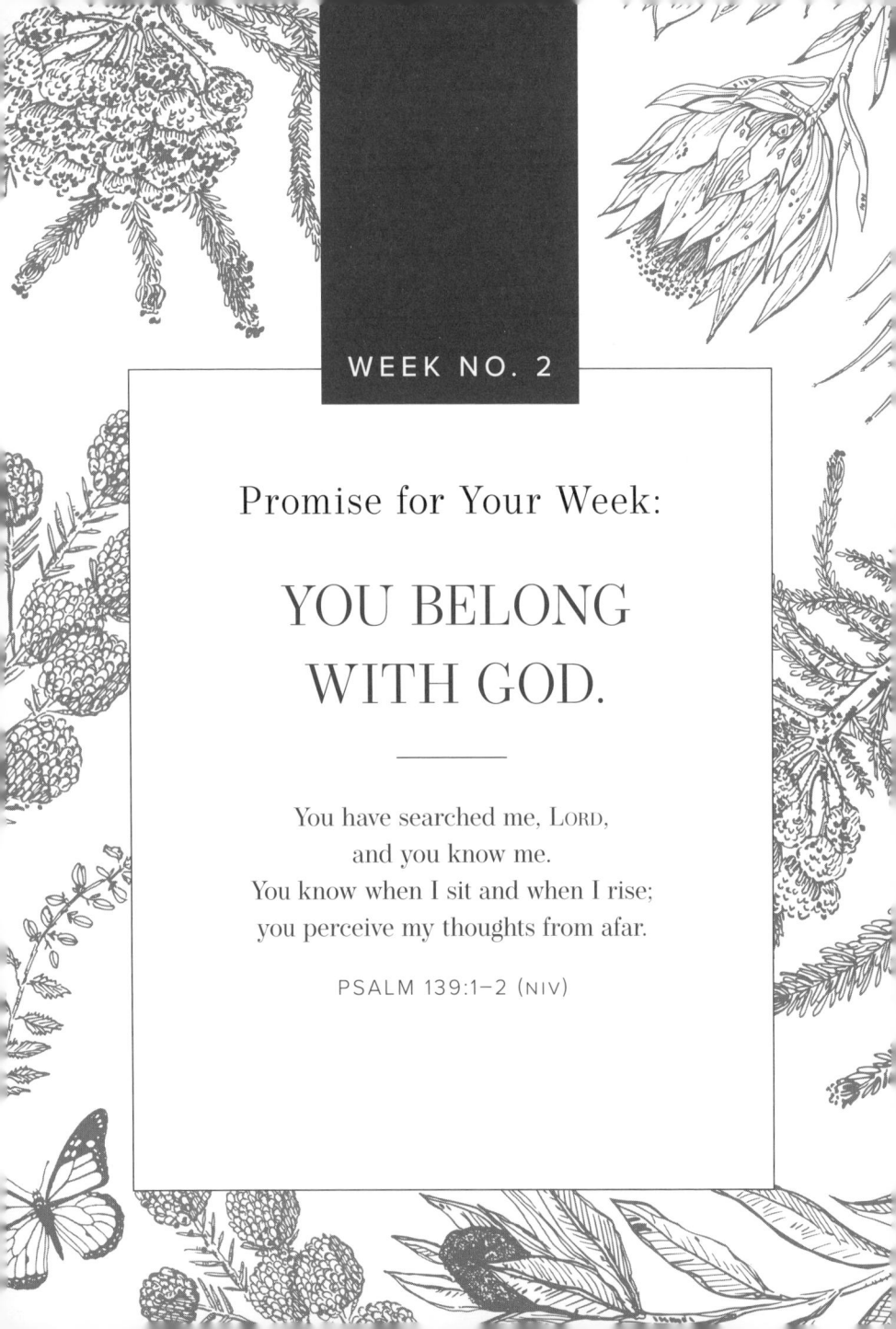

Promise for Your Week:

YOU BELONG WITH GOD.

You have searched me, Lord,
and you know me.
You know when I sit and when I rise;
you perceive my thoughts from afar.

PSALM 139:1–2 (NIV)

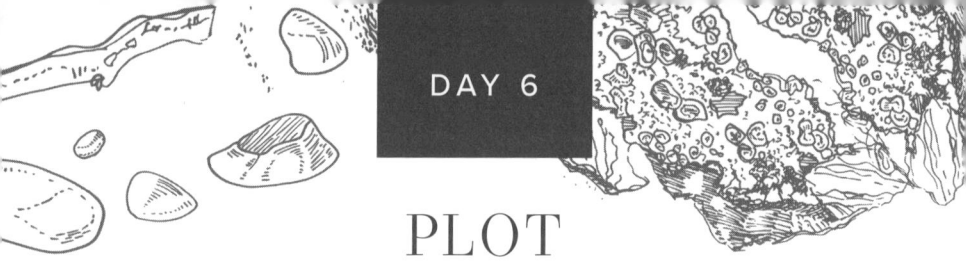

DAY 6

PLOT

One Saturday morning during football season while Tim was doing his thing as an analyst for SEC Nation on ESPN, I was killing time in the campus cafeteria when I noticed something odd. Every girl who approached the counter to grab a caffeinated drink was dressed the same way—same brand, same style from head to toe, fanny packs and all. I could've even told you what the "in" drink was at the time (sugar-free caramel). Had I somehow missed the memo? What had caused so many young women to agree about their daily decisions, right down to their wardrobe and beverage choices?

I'm certainly not immune to wanting to fit in. When I was in middle school, tie-dye was the craze. So I went to the store to buy not one, but *three* pairs of white gauchos that I personally tie-dyed myself. I wanted to be seen for my creativity while also wearing the fashionable item.

It turns out, as much as we want to be unique and individual, we also just really want to fit in. I'm sure we've all tried to fit in at some point in our lives. And unfortunately, this desire starts young. A study from the Fuller Youth Institute revealed that one of the top questions young people ask is, *Where do I fit*?[2] Maybe you're not a teenager or college student anymore, but you might still be asking that same question.

Why do we desire social approval so much? Is it because we feel deeply connected to the newest trend, or is it that we accidentally bought the same clothes as the "it" girl on campus? Do we document our vacation photos online for just ourselves? Or do we do it because we want to *belong*?

We need to realize that "fitting in" and "belonging" are two very different things. "Fitting in" is rooted in fear. It focuses on the question, *What are people going to think?* And this question leads to our endlessly working for approval and never feeling safe from sudden shifts in public opinion. This is what the world offers us.

On the other hand, to belong is to be fully known and loved. Not only known on our good days and for our good qualities but also for all our imperfections and faults—and still being loved regardless. Personally, I believe that belonging feels a lot like being loved by God.

In Romans 5:8, Paul wrote, "God demonstrates his own love for us in this: While we were still sinners, Christ died for us" (NIV). Because we are fully known and loved by the Creator of everything, we don't need to try to fit in with anyone else. We belong to the One whose opinion matters most! When Jesus was on the cross, He showed His love for us—embracing us as His family and welcoming us into a world of belonging.

PRAYER FOR YOUR DAY

Lord, teach me what it means to fully belong to You. Show me Your grace and mercy. Help me to see myself for who I am on my own, as well as who I am with You. In Jesus' name, amen.

YOU BELONG WITH GOD.

DAY 7

DIG

I met Tim's family for the first time at Thanksgiving. Football was on every TV, arts and crafts kept the young ones busy, wet footprints lined the floor from kids getting in and out of the swimming pool, and, of course, there was food. A lot of food! Tim is from a big family with a lot of boys, and they can *eat*!

So much was happening, and I just wanted to be a part of the day. I tried helping with the food, but there were more than enough competent cooks in the kitchen. And that was okay because there were many roles to be filled on this chaotic day—or so I thought.

As I skipped around from room to room, trying to take on one role and then another, I realized that everyone already had their designated roles. Fun aunt or uncle, covered. Babysitter for the young ones, covered. What about the photographer? Yep, that one was taken too. So, where did I belong?

Just when my sense of worth was starting to falter, Tim's sister noticed that I seemed a little out of place. She looked at me and said, "Don't worry. We each have our roles in the family. You'll find yours too." That simple comment, that kind gesture of love, reassured me that despite not having a clear or defined role at that moment, I was welcomed into their family, and I belonged there.

Can you remember a time you tried fitting in with a group and it didn't work out for you? What happened?

_____

_____

Can you think of a time when you felt like you truly belonged? How did that make you feel?

_____

_____

_____

What made the difference?

_____

_____

_____

A PRAYER FOR YOU FROM ME

Lord, help this beloved woman know what it means to belong with You. Teach her how to trust what You say about her and not become fixated on fitting in with others. In Jesus' name, amen.

YOU BELONG WITH GOD.

DAY 8

PLANT

When I was a little girl, I would find some of my mom's clothes and pick out what I thought was the perfect outfit based on what I had seen my mom wear. We're talking shoulder pads, oversized belts, and, of course, heels that were ten sizes too big. The only thing more mismatched than my outfit was my perception and reality. I wanted to feel important and confident in these clothes, but in reality my dress was dragging on the floor and I looked like a silly imposter.

While I may no longer wear dresses and heels that are too big for me, I still have the urge to play the part, to fit in, so that I can feel known and loved. And, yes, being known and loved are incredible things. But they are often mismatched in human relationships—with our being loved but not known or known but not loved. Tim Keller said it best: "To be loved but not known is comforting but superficial. To be known and not loved is our greatest fear."[3]

God, however, is unique. He consistently knows *and* loves you—not your perception of you, but the *real* you. So, while we may fool ourselves, we never fool God. What He knows about you goes beyond what you could ever know about yourself. He can clearly see you as the little girl in the oversized dress, pretending to be someone she's not.

In Matthew 9:10–12, the Pharisees, who were the Jewish pastors of Jesus' day, saw Jesus eating with "tax collectors and sinners." They asked His disciples why He was doing that—eating with the unclean and unwanted—and Jesus, overhearing, cut into their conversation and explained for Himself. He said, "It is not those who are healthy who need a physician, but those who are sick" (NASB1995). Not only did the lowliest—the sick—belong to Him, but He sought them out.

I don't know about you, but I'd rather be one of the sick and sit at the table with Jesus than pretend I'm healthy and be all alone. Jesus doesn't need us to be perfect; He just wants us to sit with Him because we belong with Him.

PRAYER FOR YOUR DAY

Lord, thank You for choosing to love me even when I don't love myself. Thank You for seeing me when I didn't want to look at myself and for inviting me to sit at Your table. In Jesus' name, amen.

YOU BELONG WITH GOD.

DAY 9

GROW

After Jesus was raised from the dead, He met His disciples on a beach on the coast of the Sea of Galilee. They ate breakfast together, and He talked with them about love. *Love* is a tricky word in English. People say, "I love hamburgers" as well as, "I love my wife." While both can be true, these types of love are not the same.

In ancient Greek, there are a few words that we translate into the English word *love*. Let's look at two of them: *agape* and *phileo*. *Agape* means to choose the best interest of another person and act on their behalf. It is a deep, self-sacrificing form of love. *Phileo* is a less costly kind of love, more like how we talk about our affection or friendships, and it means "to love someone like a brother."[4]

During one of the last recorded conversations between Peter and Jesus before Jesus' crucifixion, Peter told Jesus that he was willing to die for Him. But Jesus knew Peter's bold words wouldn't stand the test to come. In fact, He told Peter that he would deny knowing Him three times before morning (John 13:37–38), which is exactly what happened. Later, while Jesus was eating breakfast on the beach, He asked Peter a question: "When they had finished eating, Jesus said to Simon Peter, 'Simon son of John, do you love [*agape*] me more than these?' 'Yes, Lord,' he said, 'you know that I love [*phileo*] you.' Jesus said, 'Feed my lambs'" (John 21:15 NIV).

Peter had overpromised his love and fidelity in his previous interaction with Jesus and had failed miserably. But here on the beach, Peter finally told the truth. He knew that he couldn't live up to what

Jesus was asking—to *agape* Him—so he responded with *phileo* instead. Jesus was asking Peter if he would be willing to sacrifice himself for Him. And Peter knew he couldn't declare it.

The amazing thing about Jesus in this moment is that He reassured Peter that he still belonged to Him. Peter may have failed Him before, and he may still have been limited in his love, but Jesus met him where he was. After hearing Peter's honesty, Jesus simply said, "Feed my lambs." This was Jesus' way of telling Peter to do what he could, right now. To do what Jesus had been telling him to do the whole time they were together: Care for people.

Jesus didn't hold Peter's past over him, and He doesn't hold your past over you. He knows what you have done and still loves you. You belong with Him. Rest in the fact that Jesus isn't asking you to feel guilty about your past. He just wants you to do what He has called you to do.

PRAYER FOR YOUR DAY

Lord, thank You for Your overwhelming forgiveness. Help me live and grow in this forgiveness, looking to You—rather than the world—for guidance. In Jesus' name, amen.

YOU BELONG WITH GOD.

DAY 10

FLOURISH

Today let's read, meditate on, and memorize Psalm 139:1–2.

Yesterday we spent time on a beach with the disciples and Jesus after His resurrection. Today we're back on that same beach!

In John 21:18–19 Jesus told Peter his death would glorify God and then said, "Follow me."

Why did Peter have to die? Why didn't Jesus say this to the other disciples? These are good questions, and perhaps Peter had similar thoughts as he considered Jesus' words. He immediately asked Jesus about the disciple John, who was nearby. "Lord, what about him?" To which Jesus answered, "If I want him to remain alive until I return, *what is that to you? You must follow me*" (vv. 21–22 NIV, emphasis mine).

Jesus reminded Peter that their relationship was between them. It didn't matter what anyone else was called to do. Jesus told Peter to stop comparing himself to others and to do what He said: "Follow me."

Friend, remember that your walk with Jesus is personal. It doesn't matter what the world runs after or how God decides to use other Christians. Jesus is looking specifically at you and asking one question: Will you follow Me?

PRAYER FOR YOUR DAY

Lord, thank You for not comparing me to other people. Help me to free myself from these comparisons so I can follow You fully. In Jesus' name, amen.

YOU BELONG WITH GOD.

WEEK NO. 3

Promise for Your Week:

YOU ARE PRECIOUS TO GOD.

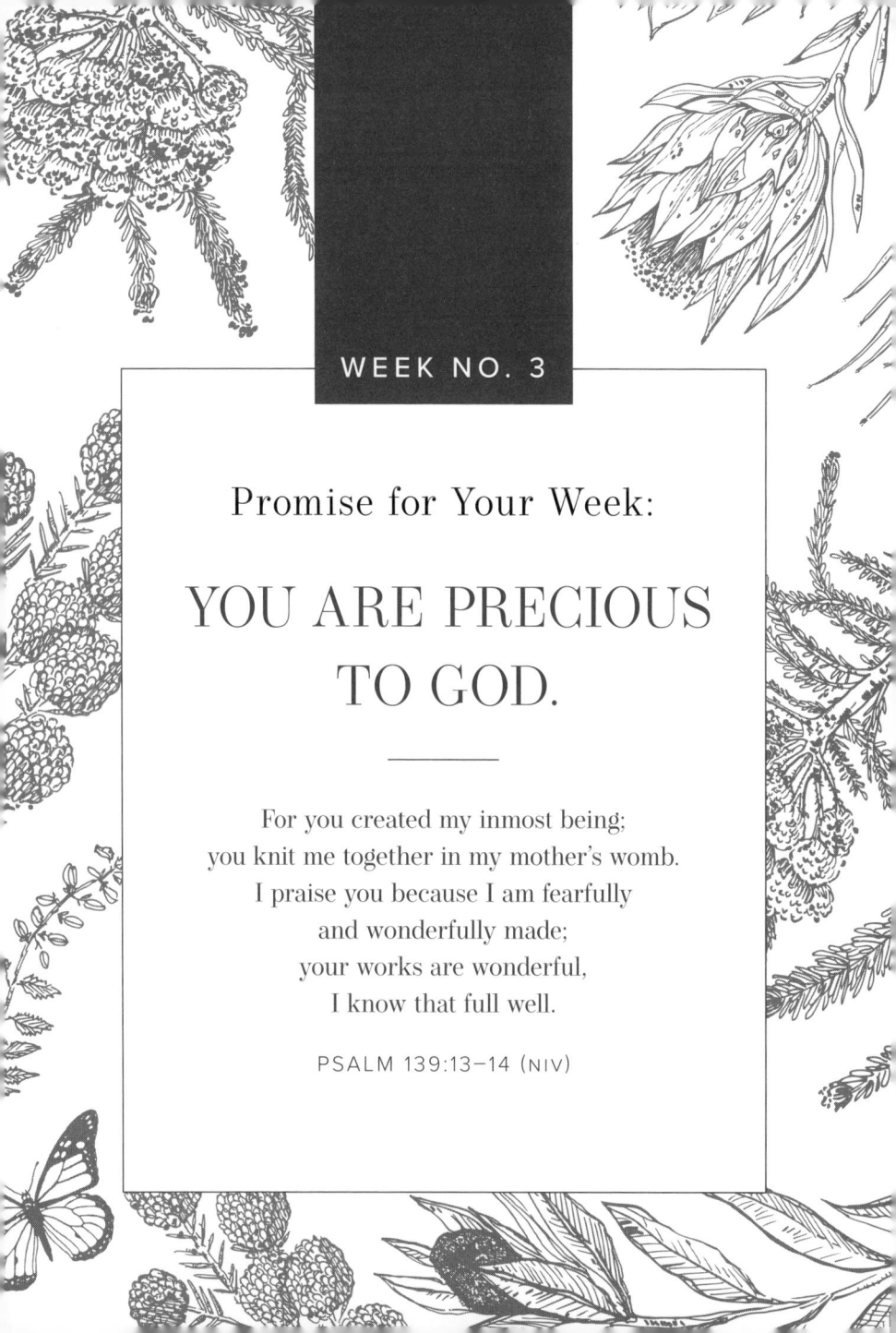

For you created my inmost being;
you knit me together in my mother's womb.
I praise you because I am fearfully
and wonderfully made;
your works are wonderful,
I know that full well.

PSALM 139:13–14 (NIV)

DAY 11

PLOT

This week we are going to put in some work as we dissect Psalm 139:13–14. These might be two of the Bible's most famous verses. Perhaps at one point your phone background or journal has even read "Fearfully and wonderfully made." But before we get to that powerful statement, let's look at how God is like a grandmother. Yes, that may sound crazy, but stay with me!

> For you created my inmost being;
> you knit me together in my mother's womb.
> (Psalm 139:13 NIV)

When I read this verse, I can't help but think of my grandmother knitting little jerseys for me when I was a child (Americans know these as "sweaters"). My grandmother made the most beautiful patterns. One of my favorite jerseys was red with a black-and-white panda on it.

Sadly, my granny was diagnosed with Alzheimer's disease a few years ago. Knowing her memory would weaken, she decided to knit me little jerseys for a future baby Tebow before she could no longer remember how to knit. She spent days knitting, and if it wasn't perfect, she'd pull it loose and rethread it to make sure it was faultless.

Her sweet act of love, even at such a fragile age, reminded me of how God knits us together in our mothers' wombs. We were knit together even more precisely and carefully than my grandmother could ever knit a jersey. Just like my grandmother planned out her patterns and blocked her designs to the inch, God also has a precise plan for our lives.

Genesis 1:27 tells us that we were created in the image of God. This means that we were not created by happenstance or a random act of nature but by the undeniable precision of God's craftsmanship. Knowing our worth and even respecting the worth of others begins when we understand that our Creator made each of us by His perfect hand. We are precious to Him.

PRAYER FOR YOUR DAY

Lord, thank You for Your care and kindness in creating me. I know that You love me, but I know only in part. Teach me what it looks like to fully live in Your love. Show me something today to help me better understand what Your love looks like. In Jesus' name, amen.

YOU ARE PRECIOUS TO GOD.

DAY 12

DIG

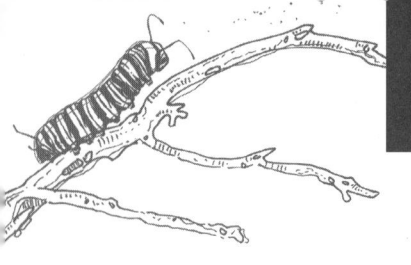

Many scholars believe that a more accurate way to define the Hebrew word for "knitted" in Psalm 139:13 would be "covered."[5] This paints a nurturing picture of God covering us with the protection of our mother's womb when we couldn't protect ourselves. Looking back, I think that's why my grandmother spent so many loving hours on those jerseys I mentioned. She wanted to cover and care for the one she loved, and jerseys were her way of doing that.

When I think about my granny, it's undeniable that she loved and valued me. The confidence and love that washes over me as I remember my grandma's love and care is overwhelming, especially because I know it was undeserved. The number of times I chose to be with my friends instead of with her, or the lack of interest I sometimes showed in things she loved—like knitting—did not stop her from caring for me.

Have you had a similar experience of undeserved care? Perhaps a friend showed up for you and covered you in kindness even though you'd been distant toward them, or maybe your husband covered you in grace after you made a backhanded comment, or perhaps a stranger gave you the available parking spot after you cut them off. God did the same thing for you—before you could ever choose to love God, He chose to love you. He cared for you in your mother's womb. He covered you with protection because He saw you as a wonderful and unique creation, created in love, by love, and for love!

What are some ways that God has "covered" you in His love, grace, and mercy, perhaps even before you were ever born?

_____

_____

_____

A PRAYER FOR YOU FROM ME

Lord, show this beautiful woman today what it means to be covered by Your grace and mercy. Do something new in her life and bless her. In Jesus' name, amen.

> **YOU ARE PRECIOUS TO GOD.**

DAY 13

PLANT

At a time when I struggled with believing that there was a plan and a purpose for my life outside of the beauty industry, I found myself on a stage next to Tim, thankful for the blinding spotlights rescuing me from having to look directly at the audience. I was asked to address the crowd and share a few motivational words. But I didn't even know how to motivate myself at the time.

I was asked a question about self-worth and confidence, so I started talking, trying to answer the question . . . but I had no idea what to say. *True beauty . . . worth . . . confidence.* I knew I had memorized an answer to a similar question before. It felt like an exam you study so hard for, memorizing the answers perfectly, but when push comes to shove, you just freeze. Finally, I recalled Psalm 139:14, a go-to verse for me, which says that I am "fearfully and wonderfully made" (NIV). *That's a good one!* I thought. *I can make something of this answer!*

I had walked out on that stage unsure of God's plan for me because I couldn't see how it practically applied to my life. But in that moment, I knew that God knew me by name, He had a plan for my life, and I was filled with infinite value. How did I know this? Because I had read it in Scripture.

Though my head was looking for the right answer, my heart was looking for the honest answer. God showed up and gave me the answer to that question—not just for the audience but for myself. I realized that I was focused on what *I* thought of me, not what *God* thought of me.

The Bible says I'm fearfully and wonderfully made, but what does that really mean? The Hebrew word for *fearfully* has a wider definition than our English word *fear*. This word can also mean "to approach someone or something with honor, respect, or heartfelt interest." And *wonderfully* in Hebrew means "extraordinary, marvelous, or something that is unexplainable."[6]

This means that you are an extraordinary, inexplicable development of God that He carefully created with an innate value that was meant to be honored and respected! You are precious to God!

PRAYER FOR YOUR DAY

Lord, teach me how to grasp and live out this beautiful truth that I am an unexplainable creation that's meant to be honored and respected. In Jesus' name, amen.

YOU ARE PRECIOUS TO GOD.

DAY 14

GROW

Yesterday we talked about how we are extraordinary creations that should be valued and respected. Self-respect is a popular idea nowadays, but how can we practice it in a biblical way?

Look around you and focus on an item that you value greatly. Meditate on all its little details. Name and describe this item below:

_____

_____

_____

Now let's consider how something is designed or made.

My mom recently got a new car. She hadn't bought a new car in over a decade, and when she first drove the vehicle, she was a little intimidated by all the new technology that her old car didn't have. Before getting behind the wheel, she wanted to make sure she knew everything about it. She read the manual front to back and even watched YouTube videos that the vehicle manufacturer produced.

If we truly want to honor and utilize something valuable in the greatest way possible, whom should we consult? The Creator! The One who knows all the details of their design. So, who is your Designer? How would you consult Him about the way you were created?

_____

_____

Psalm 111:10 says, "The fear of the LORD is the beginning of wisdom; all who follow his instructions have good insight" (CSB). And in John 14:15, Jesus says, "If you love Me, you will keep My commandments." It seems as though loving God is simpler than we often make it—*go and do*. Let's practice. In Matthew 5:37, Jesus says, "But let your 'yes' mean 'yes,' and your 'no' mean 'no'" (CSB). Here Jesus emphasizes being true to your word.

Is there any recent situation where you said you would do one thing but didn't follow through?

_____

_____

_____

The challenge today is simple: Do what Matthew 5:37 says, because true self-respect is accomplished by respecting God. If you make a commitment, keep it.

PRAYER FOR YOUR DAY

Lord, give me the courage to put Your teachings into action. Help me to trust that Your instructions are for my benefit. I want to respect myself by respecting You and Your ways. In Jesus' name, amen.

YOU ARE PRECIOUS TO GOD.

DAY 15

FLOURISH

Today let's read, meditate on, and memorize Psalm 139:13–14.

David, the author of this psalm, proclaimed that everything God has made is wonderful, especially the intricate way He designed human beings. David reinforced this truth with confidence, immediately adding, "I know that full well."

This may seem like a trivial addition, but that line is quite telling about David's headspace. He wanted the audience to know that this wasn't just a nice idea; it was a firm conviction. By declaring this statement so boldly, David was saying, "I fully trust that I am valuable to You. I believe, without hesitation, that I am wonderful in Your eyes. You are God, and I am not."

How often do I run past something God has already done, focused on asking Him for something new? Too many times! I'm quick to seek the next thing but slow to reflect on His past faithfulness.

So let's shift perspectives. Find a quiet place where you feel close to God's Spirit. Let gratitude rise as you remember instances of His faithfulness. The more we pause to recognize His work, the more confidence we build in who He is.

PRAYER FOR YOUR DAY

Lord, thank You for Your faithfulness. Thank You for staying by my side in my hurt and pain. Continue to be near to me. In Jesus' name, amen.

YOU ARE PRECIOUS TO GOD.

WEEK NO. 4

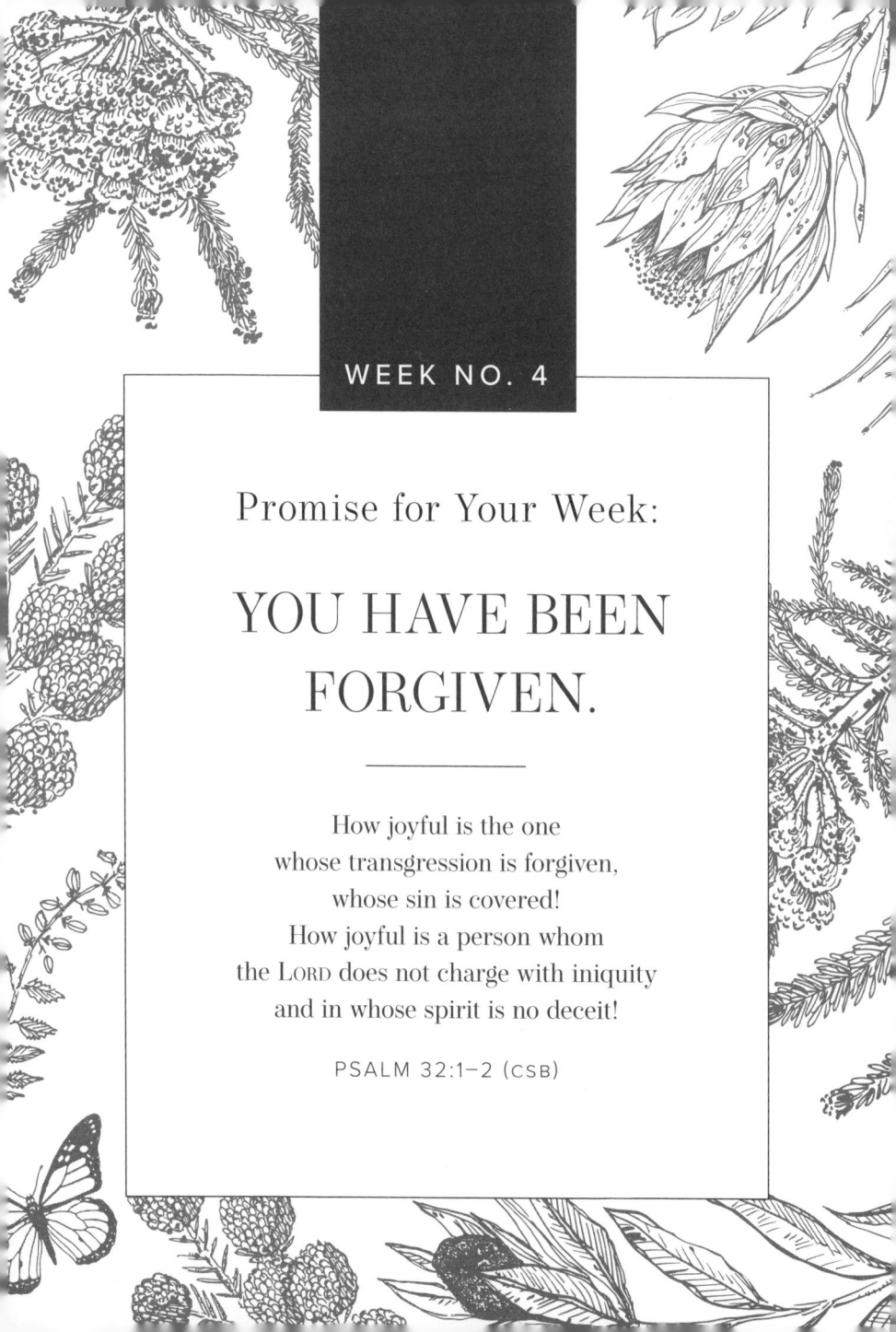

Promise for Your Week:

YOU HAVE BEEN FORGIVEN.

How joyful is the one
whose transgression is forgiven,
whose sin is covered!
How joyful is a person whom
the Lord does not charge with iniquity
and in whose spirit is no deceit!

PSALM 32:1–2 (CSB)

DAY 16

PLOT

"One of you is about to become our new Miss Universe," Steve Harvey bellowed.

Standing at center stage and shaking from adrenaline, I held the hands of Miss Colombia while Steve made his announcements. Of ninety-two contestants, we had made the final two. I was emotional just thinking about how I was one of only a few dozen women from my country ever to walk the Miss Universe stage. But now I had the chance of actually winning!

As the dramatic music built, I thought, *Surely it doesn't end here?* Steve looked at his card and announced, "The new Miss Universe is . . . *South Africa!*"

I gasped and looked around to triple-check I had heard correctly. When someone from the organization draped a sash over my shoulders and handed me a bouquet of colorful flowers, I knew my little-girl dream had come true. I couldn't help but tear up. My heart was so full, and my cheeks hurt because I couldn't stop smiling! I had just become the sixty-sixth Miss Universe.

Reflecting on that unforgettable moment brings back all the feels. The bright lights, the goose bumps, the cheering crowd, the waving flags, the *joy* of hearing my country being announced as winner—it was a dream come true in every sense of the word.

But as incredible as that moment was, it pales in comparison to the *joy of forgiveness* I have because of my faith in Christ! In Psalm 32:1, David wrote, "How *joyful* is the one whose transgression is forgiven, whose sin is covered!" (CSB). In the New Testament, Paul echoed David, saying, "Oh, what joy for those whose disobedience is forgiven, whose sins are put out of sight. Yes, what joy for those whose record the LORD has cleared of sin" (Romans 4:7–8 NLT). The Bible suggests that the right response to knowing that our sin is completely forgiven when we choose to trust Christ is . . . *joy*!

Sit in that for a moment. Think about one of your most exciting, most enjoyable experiences. Are all the feels coming back? If they are, now think about this: As awesome as that moment was, how does it feel to know the joy of being forgiven of all past, present, and future sins? It is far greater!

Your memorable experience, as well as my winning moment on stage, are just moments in time. But this joy, tied to our forgiveness, is eternal. It can never be taken away from us because Jesus' victory can never be undone. Forgiveness in Christ is a surpassing joy that exceeds all circumstances because it's a joy rooted in what Jesus' death and resurrection fully accomplished for us. It's a joy that is available to us every single day, and it's a joy worthy of our applause and celebration!

PRAYER FOR YOUR DAY

God, thank You for the incredible gift of forgiveness. Help me to come humbly before You, acknowledging my sins and receiving Your mercy and grace. Fill my heart with abundant joy as I experience the freedom that comes from being forgiven and restored in Your love. In Jesus' name, amen.

YOU HAVE BEEN FORGIVEN.

DAY 17

DIG

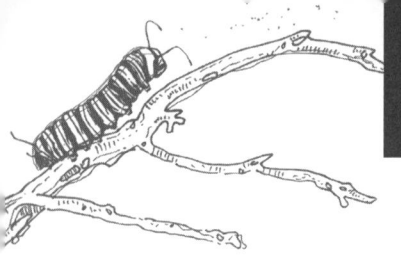

As I mentioned yesterday, joy is our right response to knowing we're completely forgiven in Christ. Sure, our human nature will continue to sin, but 1 John 1:9 tells us, "If we confess our sins [to God], He is faithful and righteous, so that He will forgive us our sins and cleanse us from all unrighteousness." Amen! I'm so grateful that the forgiveness God offers was not just a onetime thing at the moment of our salvation. No, it is something He continuously offers when we bring our messes and chaos to Him. He takes our sin and makes us clean. What a trade!

The problem, however, is that we sometimes find ourselves burdened by our mistakes, carrying the weight of shame and guilt. Instead of bringing our sin to the Lord, we keep it hidden from Him and others. This is nothing new; even David tried to keep quiet about his sin (Psalm 32:3). But as I'm sure you've experienced, nothing productive comes from hiding. A friend once shared with me, "You are only as sick as your secrets and as healthy as you are honest." Today I invite you into deeper honesty with God. The joy is in forgiveness, so to receive it, we need to ask for it.

Here are a few questions to help you think through forgiveness:

What specific actions or behaviors are weighing heavily on your heart that you could take to God? What underlying thoughts or attitudes have contributed to these actions or behaviors?

_____

_____

Is there any area of your life you've avoided sharing with God or those close to you because of shame or guilt?

_____

_____

Are there secrets you hold that weigh you down or make you feel embarrassed and unworthy of God's love?

_____

_____

A PRAYER FOR YOU FROM ME

Father God, we are quick to forget Your love for us! As this reader comes humbly before You, may Your kindness cover all shame and Your grace cover all sin. May darkness be exposed, and may this reader experience true joy and freedom by living in Your light! In Jesus' name, amen.

YOU HAVE BEEN FORGIVEN.

DAY 18

PLANT

How are you feeling today? Yesterday's devo may have been a gut-wrenching time of reflection. Digging up pain, sharing secrets, and bringing into the light things we may not want to share is not a comfortable process. However, though we may not like it, it's worth it. In Psalm 32:5, David's words remind us of the beautiful promise we're given when we acknowledge sin:

> I acknowledged my sin to You,
> And I did not hide my guilt;
> I said, "I will confess my wrongdoings to the Lord";
> And You forgave the guilt of my sin.

When we humbly come before the Lord, hope and healing have the chance to impact our lives. One of the best examples of this is found in Luke 5:17–26.

In Jesus' first year of public ministry, He found Himself teaching to a full house in Capernaum. Many had gathered to hear Him speak, coming from every village of Galilee, Judea, and some even from Jerusalem (roughly a 120-mile trek!). In Mark's gospel, we're told that there was "no longer space [in the house], not even near the door" (2:2). The room was packed!

As Jesus was teaching, "some men were carrying a man on a stretcher who was paralyzed; and they were trying to bring him in and to set him down in front of Him. But when they did not find any way to bring him in because of the crowd, they went up on the roof and let him down through the tiles with his stretcher, into the middle of the crowd, in front of Jesus" (Luke 5:18–19).

This story is included in all three Synoptic Gospels.[7] However, only in Luke's gospel is it explicitly noted that the men put the paralyzed man *in front of* Jesus. I don't believe that inclusion was an accident. I believe Luke was trying to tell us that when we get in front of Jesus, something special can happen.

And something special did happen. Seeing the faith and all the effort of those men to help their friend, Jesus said to the paralytic, "Friend, your sins are forgiven. . . . Get up, and pick up your stretcher, and go home" (Luke 5:20, 24). Immediately the man got up and went home rejoicing!

In front of the whole crowd, Jesus made His true power known—He not only had the ability to heal, but He had the divine power to *forgive* sin. As you go about your day and the rest of the week, will you, like the paralytic man, be desperate to get *in front of* Jesus?

PRAYER FOR YOUR DAY

Father, You are the great Healer and Forgiver! Put people in my life that push me toward Jesus. May my heart be ever so desperate to get in front of You, to meet with You, to enjoy Your presence. Thank You for giving me access to You. Amen.

YOU HAVE BEEN FORGIVEN.

DAY 19

GROW

There's an interesting parallel between Psalm 32 and Luke 5, as both address paralysis. In Psalm 32, David experienced a sense of being spiritually paralyzed from the effects of hiding his sin. But when he confessed it before God, he received forgiveness and rejoiced because of it. In Luke 5, the man on the stretcher was physically paralyzed. When he was placed before Jesus, Jesus forgave him of his sin, healed him, and the man ran home rejoicing.

In both passages, we see three things at play: some form of paralysis, forgiveness of sin, and a response of joy.

	Paralyzed	Forgiveness of sin	Rejoicing
Psalm 32	Spiritually (vv. 3–4)	Then I acknowledged my sin to you and did not conceal my iniquity. I said, "I will confess my transgressions to the Lord," and you forgave the guilt of my sin. (v. 5 CSB)	Be glad in the Lord and rejoice, you righteous ones; shout for joy, all you upright in heart. (v. 11 CSB)
Luke 5:17–26	Physically (v. 18)	Seeing their faith, He said, "Friend, your sins are forgiven you." (v. 20)	Immediately he got up before them, and picked up what he had been lying on, and went home glorifying God. (v. 25)

If we want to experience the joy and rejoicing that come from forgiveness, we'll have to face and acknowledge our sin, which otherwise keeps us "paralyzed." The author of Hebrews commanded, "Let's rid ourselves of every obstacle and the sin which so easily entangles us" (Hebrews 12:1). Here, sin is obviously not idle; it can capture us. If we are not quick to confess, we risk allowing our sin to take us captive and bury us in shame. Our right response to sin is to trust that God forgives when we bring it to Him and to rejoice in the fact that He is faithful.

God joyfully offers forgiveness, so we should joyfully receive it.

PRAYER FOR YOUR DAY

Thank You, Father, for doing something I cannot do myself—forgive my own sin. You never stop forgiving when I ask. Please give me a renewed lens to recognize my sin and a new joy that more fully appreciates the forgiveness You offer. In Jesus' name, amen.

YOU HAVE BEEN FORGIVEN.

DAY 20

FLOURISH

Today let's read, meditate on, and memorize Psalm 32:1–2 (CSB):

> How joyful is the one
> whose transgression is forgiven,
> whose sin is covered!
> How joyful is a person whom
> the LORD does not charge with iniquity
> and in whose spirit is no deceit!

You can walk with God today and every day by embracing honesty and humility. Instead of hiding your shortcomings or pretending to have it all together, be quick to lay your sins before God. True joy, strength, and healing come when you honestly acknowledge your weaknesses. The more you embrace the reality of being fully forgiven, the more confident you will become in your identity as a beloved daughter of the King.

In what ways can regular confession strengthen your faith and empower you to live boldly for Christ?

A PRAYER FOR YOU FROM ME

Dear Lord, as Your daughter lays bare her heart before You, acknowledging her need for Your forgiveness and grace, allow her to experience the liberating power of Your love. In Jesus' name, amen.

YOU HAVE BEEN FORGIVEN.

WEEK NO. 5

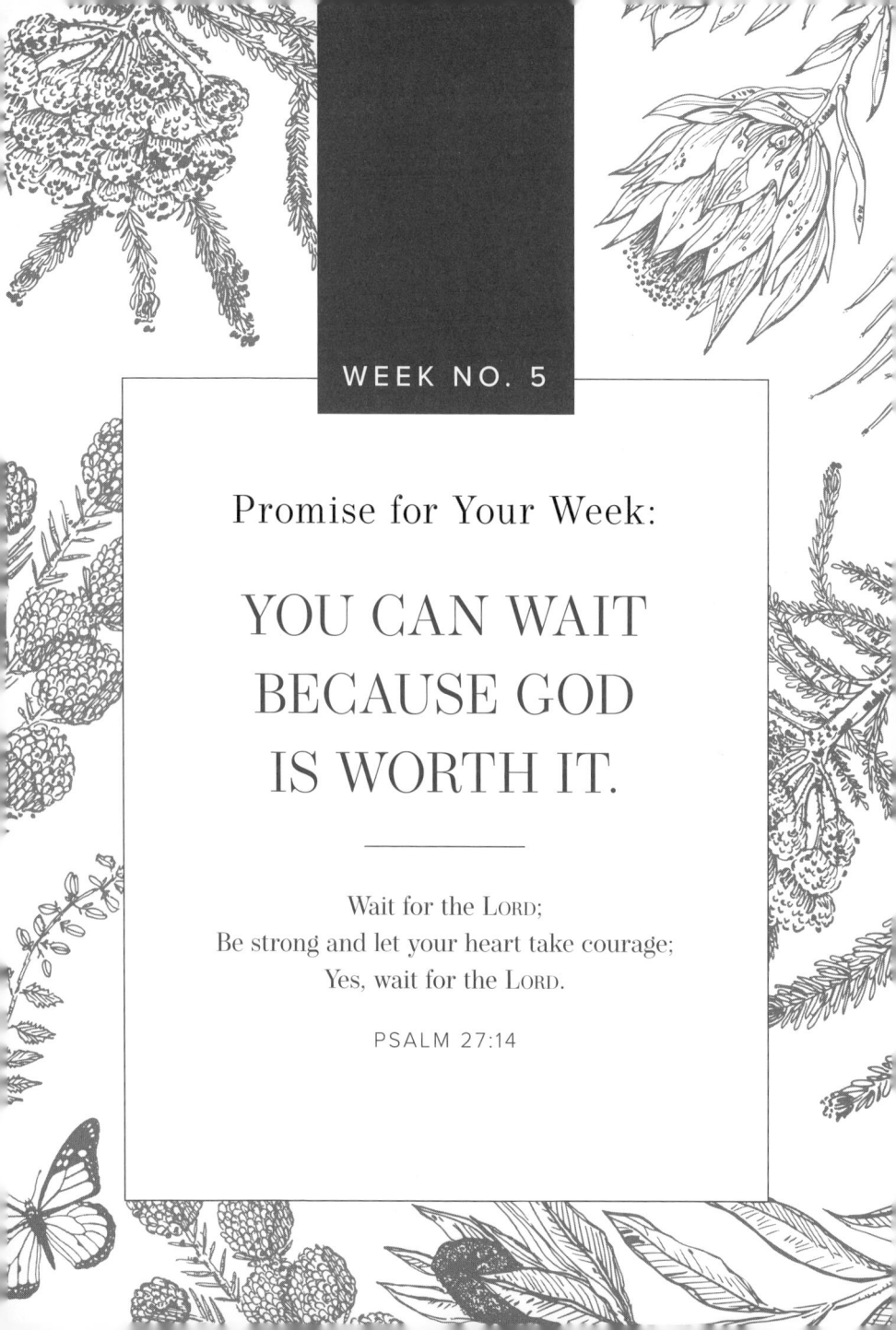

Promise for Your Week:

YOU CAN WAIT BECAUSE GOD IS WORTH IT.

Wait for the Lord;
Be strong and let your heart take courage;
Yes, wait for the Lord.

PSALM 27:14

DAY 21

PLOT

After relinquishing my Miss Universe crown to the next winner, I entered a brutal waiting period. I had no idea what to do next. So much of my life up to that point had been about pageant competitions, and now that it was over, life felt hard, confusing, and out of sync. I didn't know where to live—not just which city, but even which continent. I thought about moving from New York back to South Africa to be with my family, but Tim was in the States, and I didn't want to be that far away from him. With all these unknowns and my identity shifting, I constantly questioned my life's purpose and felt stuck. Even small successes required a huge effort. I had few friends nearby, and Tim was playing baseball hours away, which made the world feel quite lonely. This gave me little energy to plan my future. Needless to say, I was *waiting* for change, but I wasn't seeing it.

Maybe you can relate. Have you ever been in a season where you didn't have clarity on what to do? Or did you want something so badly but never seemed to get any closer to having it? It's frustrating and certainly can create anxiety, questions, and discontent.

Most of my life I've viewed *waiting* as a negative word. It feels unproductive and like nothing is happening. There are often more questions than answers, and those periods seem to last forever. But I've discovered that waiting can be a *good* thing. There are benefits to waiting. Often it's an opportunity to see life on God's terms. Let's look at it differently: *What if waiting is an invitation to experience God more deeply?*

Psalm 27:14 says, "Wait for the LORD; Be strong and let your heart take courage; Yes, wait for the LORD."

This verse implies that waiting is not just about being patient; it's about having active faith and trusting in God's timing, even when we can't see the bigger picture.

After my waiting season in New York, I learned that God was using that time to shape me, to build my character, and to teach me to rely on Him rather than my own understanding (Proverbs 3:5–6).

Over the next few days, I hope to challenge your idea of what it means to wait and to encourage you into its beautiful mystery. Waiting may not be fun, but I'm learning that it is *worth it*.

PRAYER FOR YOUR DAY

Heavenly Father, in seasons of waiting, give me patience and strength to trust in Your perfect timing. Help me to see these moments as opportunities to deepen my faith and grow closer to You. Strengthen my character. I believe You want to do something in me! I'm available for what that is. May Your will be done in me. In Jesus' name, amen.

YOU CAN WAIT BECAUSE GOD IS WORTH IT.

DAY 22

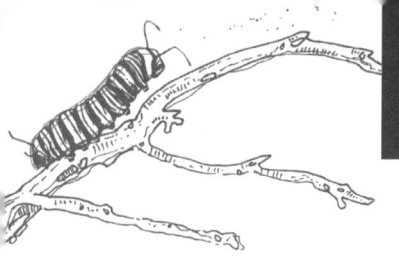

DIG

Yesterday I briefly shared one of my waiting seasons after handing over the Miss Universe crown. During that time, many days felt worse than just waiting—they felt *wasted*.

Today I want you to reflect on your own life. Whether you were waiting to receive a college admission letter, the double line on a pregnancy test, or the results from a recent doctor visit, write out a time when you struggled to "wait for the Lord."

What questions were you asking? What emotions did you feel? What doubts were you experiencing?

_____

_____

_____

_____

_____

_____

I'm realizing that to live is to *wait*. We can't escape it. Everybody experiences it in some way at some point. However, waiting doesn't mean doing nothing. It's not an excuse to sit on our heels and avoid responsibility. I'm always convicted when my husband points out that we don't usually hear stories about God radically moving in someone's life when they're watching Netflix! Sure, God is God. He can do what He wants. But the point is that not much happens when we're stagnant.

Tomorrow we'll explore a few practical things to proactively navigate the *wait*. Remember, even in your waiting, God is working and wants you to grow through it.

A PRAYER FOR YOU FROM ME

Father God, may Your loving-kindness encourage this reader. You are so far and above time—not constrained by its limits, but rather, in control of it all. Seasons of waiting can feel isolating and lonely, but I ask You to make Your presence known today. Be ever so near, and may Your almighty power bring peace to any uncertain situation. In Jesus' name, amen.

> **YOU CAN WAIT BECAUSE GOD IS WORTH IT.**

DAY 23

PLANT

To wait well implies a willingness. In one of my favorite Bible stories, Ruth the Moabite becomes a widow in a foreign land. After choosing to move to Bethlehem with her mother-in-law, Naomi, Ruth decided to occupy her time in a barley field, collecting grain scraps behind the harvesters (Ruth 2:2).[8] Because of Ruth's work ethic and loyalty to Naomi, she found favor with the field owner, Boaz. And long story short, Boaz took a liking to Ruth and the two eventually got married.

What I love about the first part of Ruth's story is that instead of sitting around waiting for God to bring her friends or a new spouse in a new city, she got up and went to work. Despite all the possible unknowns, Ruth turned what could have been a miserable waiting season into a *willing* season. Inspired by Ruth's willingness, I want to share two practical ways we can be willing while waiting.

1. **Serve someone.** Perhaps this is cliché, but it's also beneficial. When our minds are constantly focused on how not to be in our current waiting situation, it is easy to get stuck on thinking about ourselves. Please hear this: Get the focus off yourself. There are so many hurting people waiting for someone to help them. Perhaps in your willingness to serve through your waiting season, you can become an answer to someone else's prayer.

2. **Lean into a Christ-centered community and ask for help.** Living isolated isn't good for anyone. My pastor likes to say that when we live in the dark (i.e., live isolated), we get our butts kicked by the Enemy. He's not wrong. In waiting seasons, our pride can get in the way of being vulnerable or asking for help. We need friends who can be sounding boards or point us back to the truth when we're discouraged.

I know some of this is easier said than done. But as you navigate your waiting season, remember it's not a time to be passive. It's a time to be proactive.

PRAYER FOR YOUR DAY

Dear heavenly Father, thank You for Ruth's example and her willingness to work through her waiting season. Help us to serve others selflessly, seek a supportive community, and remain active and willing in our times of waiting. May we grow closer to You and find purpose in these seasons. In Jesus' name, amen.

> **YOU CAN WAIT BECAUSE GOD IS WORTH IT.**

DAY 24

GROW

Perhaps you've heard the phrase "It was worth the wait" but have a hard time believing that could be true. Waiting can feel like a frustrating pause in our lives. However, it's often a period of preparation and growth that puts many things into perspective.

After my Miss Universe reign ended in 2018, I was thrilled to be invited to film a project in South America. It was the first big gig I was offered after Miss Universe. But my excitement was cut short when the production was delayed indefinitely. So, instead, I returned to South Africa feeling disappointed that I wasn't able to be on set. However, because I went home, I got to celebrate my sister Franje's thirteenth birthday with our family. Franje had cerebellar agenesis and couldn't swallow food, so we had cupcakes instead of a cake. Little did I know that this was going to be her last birthday with us. Two months later, God called Franje home.

In 2020 I got a call that filming for the postponed project was back on! We were scheduled to start shooting on what would have been Franje's fourteenth birthday. The morning of the start date, I was astonished to find that the same kind of cupcakes we had at Franje's party the previous year were in the breakfast line, of all places. I was overwhelmed and couldn't help but laugh at the situation. It felt like she was right there with me. That morning, I got to celebrate my sister's first heavenly birthday. It was as if God winked at me through those cupcakes to remind me that He was in control and that I could trust Him with what seemed like an interruption in my life.

As we wait, it's important to stay focused on the truth that God is with us in every season. Those little God winks can keep us going by reminding us that we are not waiting in vain. Each moment is a chance to grow, to learn, and to prepare us for the incredible plans that God has in store.

The waiting is worth it because it builds character, deepens our faith, and prepares us to experience God in new ways. Embrace this time, trust in His timing, and believe that every setback is a setup for something greater. And if you take the time to be present in your waiting, you might just catch your own little God-wink moment along the way.

As Psalm 27:14 encourages us, "Wait for the Lord; Be strong and let your heart take courage; Yes, wait for the Lord."

PRAYER FOR YOUR DAY

Dear God, thank You for the seasons of waiting and preparation. Help me to trust in Your perfect timing and use these times to grow closer to You. Remind me that every waiting period is an opportunity for growth, and give me the strength to flourish in every season. May I always have courage and wait for You, knowing that Your plans are good. In Jesus' name, amen.

YOU CAN WAIT BECAUSE GOD IS WORTH IT.

DAY 25

FLOURISH

Today let's read, meditate on, and memorize Psalm 27:14.

Sometimes the most practical way to wait on the Lord is to slow down on purpose and sit in His presence. Spend the next few minutes to *slow*, *sit*, and *rest* in God's presence. Find a quiet spot that's free of distractions. Set a timer for five minutes. Ask God to clear your mind of distractions and highlight what He wants you to focus on.

What came to mind? A phrase? A scripture? Maybe nothing—and that's okay too. If you're unsure whether God is speaking to you, check the idea against the Bible. If the Bible supports it, great! If not, set it aside to share with other believers.

I like to think of discerning God's voice as a triangle: the Bible, other believers, and prayer. God often speaks through these three avenues. Using them together helps confirm His direction. Next time something enters your heart when you're waiting on God, test it through this method. You might be surprised how much God reveals when Scripture, wise counsel, and prayer come together!

PRAYER FOR YOU FROM ME

Lord, thank You for waiting seasons. Please work in this reader's life as she seeks Your will above her own. Help her to trust Your ways even in her fear and unbelief. In Jesus' name, amen.

YOU CAN WAIT BECAUSE GOD IS WORTH IT.

WEEK NO. 6

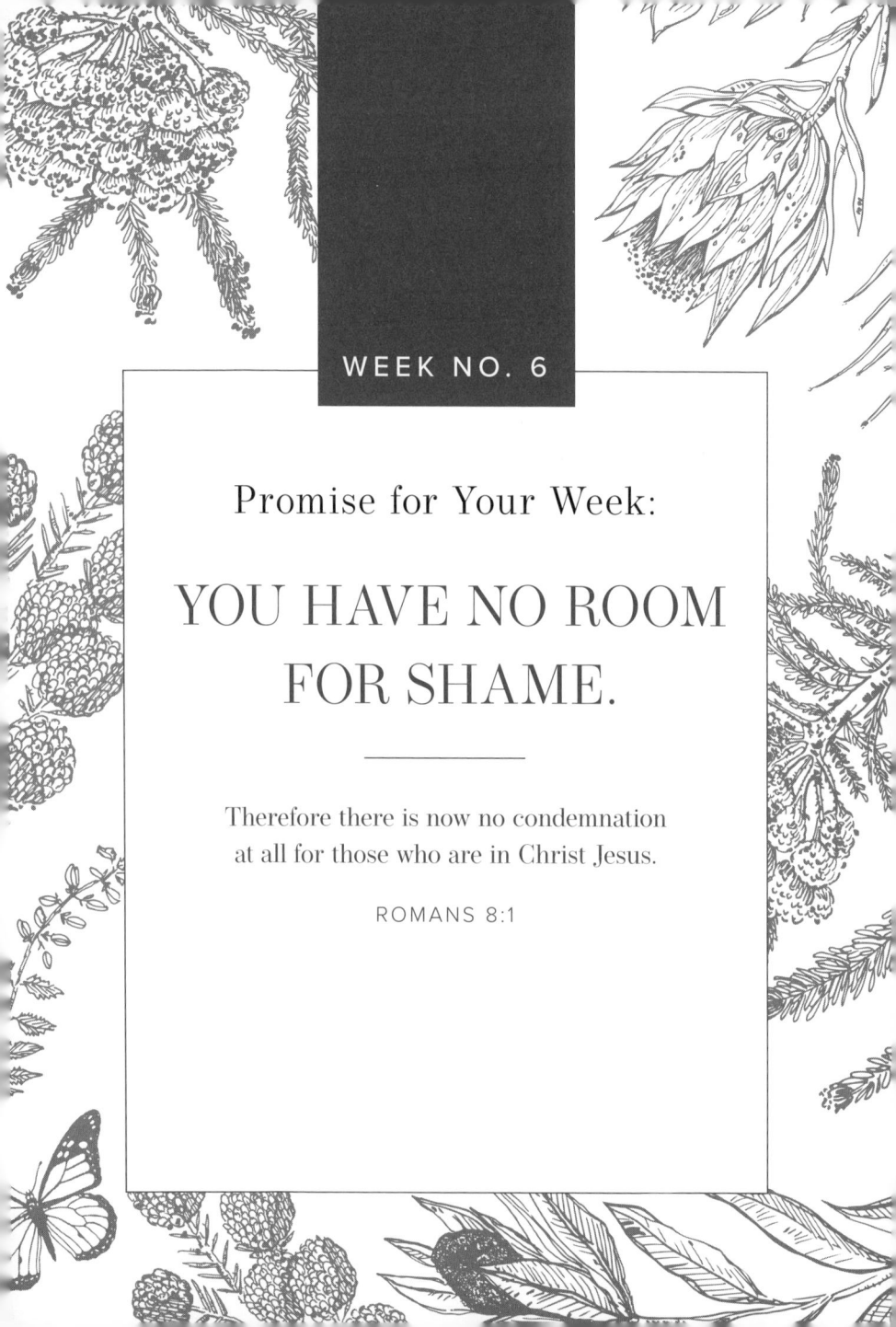

Promise for Your Week:

YOU HAVE NO ROOM FOR SHAME.

Therefore there is now no condemnation
at all for those who are in Christ Jesus.

ROMANS 8:1

DAY 26

PLOT

I was sprawled on the airport floor, juggling gowns, heels, and the remnants of my Miss Universe glam, trying to downsize my six-suitcase life into the one-suitcase airline limit. All eyes were on me, including those of Tim and a host of traveling spectators, which was increasing in size by the minute. They curiously watched me. Me, the sweaty, fully glammed woman on the floor surrounded by clothing and toiletry mayhem.

What was going on? I had just finished my tenure as Miss Universe, crowning the new young lady who would carry the prestigious title for the next year. What I didn't realize when I packed for Thailand was that I would not be able to take my six bags with me on my return. It was a whirlwind. Tim, my knight in shining armor, had cut a family trip short and flown from Israel to Thailand just to cheer me on as I passed on the Miss Universe crown. We were a fairly new couple, and he was already scoring major boyfriend points. Now, as we tried to hurry through Bangkok's airport, I was mortified. In a check-in crisis, we wrestled with six bursting suitcases, which included a mountain of Miss Universe programs—forty to be exact.

No longer the current Miss Universe, I was forced to condense my six suitcases into one in order to meet the airline's requirements. I haphazardly transferred my belongings, but the evidence of my yearlong reign stubbornly refused to cooperate. As we went through security, more chaos ensued as the bottom of Tim's garment bag, into which he had managed to squeeze the programs, burst open. And there they were: my Miss Universe moments scattered across the floor.

In that moment, scrambling to gather them off the floor, I realized my Miss Universe chapter had truly ended. More than simply a chaotic airport journey, this moment was a humiliating illustration of my detonated identity. And that embarrassment uncovered my deepest shame about who I *wasn't* anymore without having a clue about who I *was*.

Shame has an awful way of showing up uninvited, adding to how terrible we already feel. Maybe you've felt its presence as you remembered doing the thing you promised you'd never do again. Or perhaps you felt it when someone pointed out a flaw, your less-than-stellar effort, or a deficiency. Or maybe you've wondered if the traumatic thing that happened was actually your fault.

This week I want to give you hope by reminding you that shame has no seat at your table. No matter what you've done or haven't done, Jesus is your cheerleader, not a shaming dictator. Remember, you are a beloved child of God. His love for you is unbreakable.

PRAYER FOR YOUR DAY

Lord, I invite You into the places I feel unloved and unworthy. Shine Your light, love me in my darkness, and tenderly guide me to Your grace where I find acceptance and healing. In Jesus' name, amen.

> **YOU HAVE NO ROOM FOR SHAME.**

DAY 27

DIG

The dictionary defines shame as "the painful feeling arising from the consciousness of something dishonorable, improper, ridiculous, etc., done by oneself or another."[9] I like how Brené Brown puts it: "the intensely painful feeling or experience of believing that we are flawed and therefore unworthy of love and belonging."[10]

Shame often stems from our deepest fears and insecurities, magnified by past mistakes, societal pressures, and the unrealistic standards we set for ourselves. Shame thrives in the space between who we are and who we think we should be. It's fed by comparison, criticism, and the hidden wounds of our stories.

Take a moment to reflect on a recent time when you felt overwhelmed by shame.

What triggered these feelings, and how did they affect your perception of yourself?

_____

_____

_____

How does your struggle with shame affect your relationship with others and with God?

_____

_____

_____

A PRAYER FOR YOU FROM ME

Dear heavenly Father, wrap this precious soul in Your love and free her from the grip of shame. Grant her the courage to face her shadows, knowing You walk beside her always. Renew her spirit, fill her heart with grace, and remind her that she is beautifully made in Your image. In Jesus' name, amen.

YOU HAVE NO ROOM FOR SHAME.

DAY 28

PLANT

Shame can quickly cloud our perception of ourselves and our relationship with God. Yet, amid our struggles, we can rest in the liberating and game-changing truth of Romans 8:1(NIV):

> Therefore, there is now no condemnation for those who are in Christ Jesus.

To be condemned means to be guilty; to deserve punishment. And shame fuels the voice of condemnation, shouting things like, "You're guilty," "You don't deserve forgiveness," "If only they saw you on your worst day!" And to be fair, without Christ, rejection and condemnation would be our story. However, that is not our story when we accept Jesus as our Savior.

Romans 8:1 reminds us that as followers of Christ, we are not defined by our past mistakes, our shortcomings, or the labels the world may place upon us. Instead, God sees us through the lens of Jesus' sacrifice—forgiven, redeemed, and deeply loved. We are invited to view our identity through a different perspective—one that is rooted in the unconditional love and acceptance of Jesus Christ.

In Paul's Greco-Roman culture, competition was a big deal, which we see a glimpse of in his writings in the New Testament, as he often used sports metaphors. These competitions were not only physical contests but also carried social, political, and religious weight. The most important games included the Isthmian, Nemean, and Pythian games. Athletes who lost didn't just suffer the sting of public defeat but were also severely shamed. The Greek philosopher Epictetus, who lived from AD 50 to 135, reflected on this when he wrote:

> In the [games] you cannot just be beaten and then depart, but first of all, you will be disgraced not only before the people of Athens or Sparta or Nicopolis but before the whole world. In the second place, if you withdraw without sufficient reason, you will be whipped. And this whipping comes after your training which involves thirst and broiling heat and swallowing handfuls of sand.[11]

Yikes! While we in modern times will probably not be whipped or forced to eat sand, many of us can relate to the pain of self-condemnation. Let this encourage you: In Jesus, condemnation doesn't exist. It's not part of the gift of salvation, nor does it follow on the heels of our missteps or sin. Freedom in Jesus is yours today, right now! No matter how heavily the weight of shame or condemnation may rest on your shoulders, it is not yours to carry.

PRAYER FOR YOUR DAY

God, I thank You for the freedom You have given us through sacrificing Your only Son. I often need reminding that You didn't come to earth to punish or make us cower in the shadow of shame, but You have called us to live in Your love. Thank You that You are always for me. In Jesus' name, amen.

YOU HAVE NO ROOM FOR SHAME.

DAY 29

GROW

Do you ever try to avoid God or slowly distance yourself from Him because you don't feel like you're enough, or you messed up again, or you're distraught because the life you worked so hard to build has shattered? We need to remember that when we isolate ourselves from Him, our self-condemning thoughts grow louder and louder by the day.

Shame tells us we're unworthy of God's presence and love, but the gospel tells a different story—one of unconditional love and open arms. James 4:8 says, "Come close to God and He will come close to you." He doesn't require our perfection, nor does He care if we're a blubbering mess. God yearns for our presence!

Instead of allowing shame to boss you around, let it be the very thing that draws you into God's presence. When we are near to Him, we are reminded of our true identity as children of God, whom He loves without condition or limit.

Don't allow shame to dictate your distance from the Divine. Instead, use it to propel you into His embrace. In God you are not meant to be hidden in shadows but transformed in light.

When we turn to Him, we become marked not by our imperfections but by His perfect love. So, friend, stop running. Turn toward the One who has been pursuing you all along and find rest in His relentless grace. The Enemy has no power to whisper condemnation in your ear. You have been set free!

PRAYER FOR YOUR DAY

Heavenly Father, draw me closer to You. Fill my heart with Your presence and love so I might find comfort and companionship in You alone. Teach me to seek You in all moments, knowing You are always near. In Jesus' name, amen.

> **YOU HAVE NO ROOM FOR SHAME.**

DAY 30

FLOURISH

Today let's read, meditate on, and memorize Romans 8:1.

Shame can come from many sources. Its overwhelming presence can creep up when we've done something wrong and we know it. But shame can also appear when we've done nothing wrong, like when we feel guilty about not measuring up or when someone convinces us that something is our fault. And if we're not careful, we start to believe the lie that shame is just something we must live with.

If your shame struggle comes from sin you're living in, the remedy is simple. Confess it, turn from it, and receive God's forgiveness. No matter what you've done, no matter how long you've been doing it, God forgives. Remember, shame and conviction are not the same. Conviction comes from God; shame does not.

So ask yourself, is shame gripping your heart today? If it's not tied to unconfessed sin, it doesn't belong there. Shut it down by dwelling on the truth of Scripture. When shame starts whispering lies, speak God's promises out loud. Because the Enemy wants you stuck in shame, but God wants you walking in freedom.

PRAYER FOR YOUR DAY

Lord, Thank You for Your forgiveness. Thank You that in You there is no condemnation. Help me to trust that You truly love and want the best for me. In Jesus' name I pray, amen.

YOU HAVE NO ROOM FOR SHAME.

WEEK NO. 7

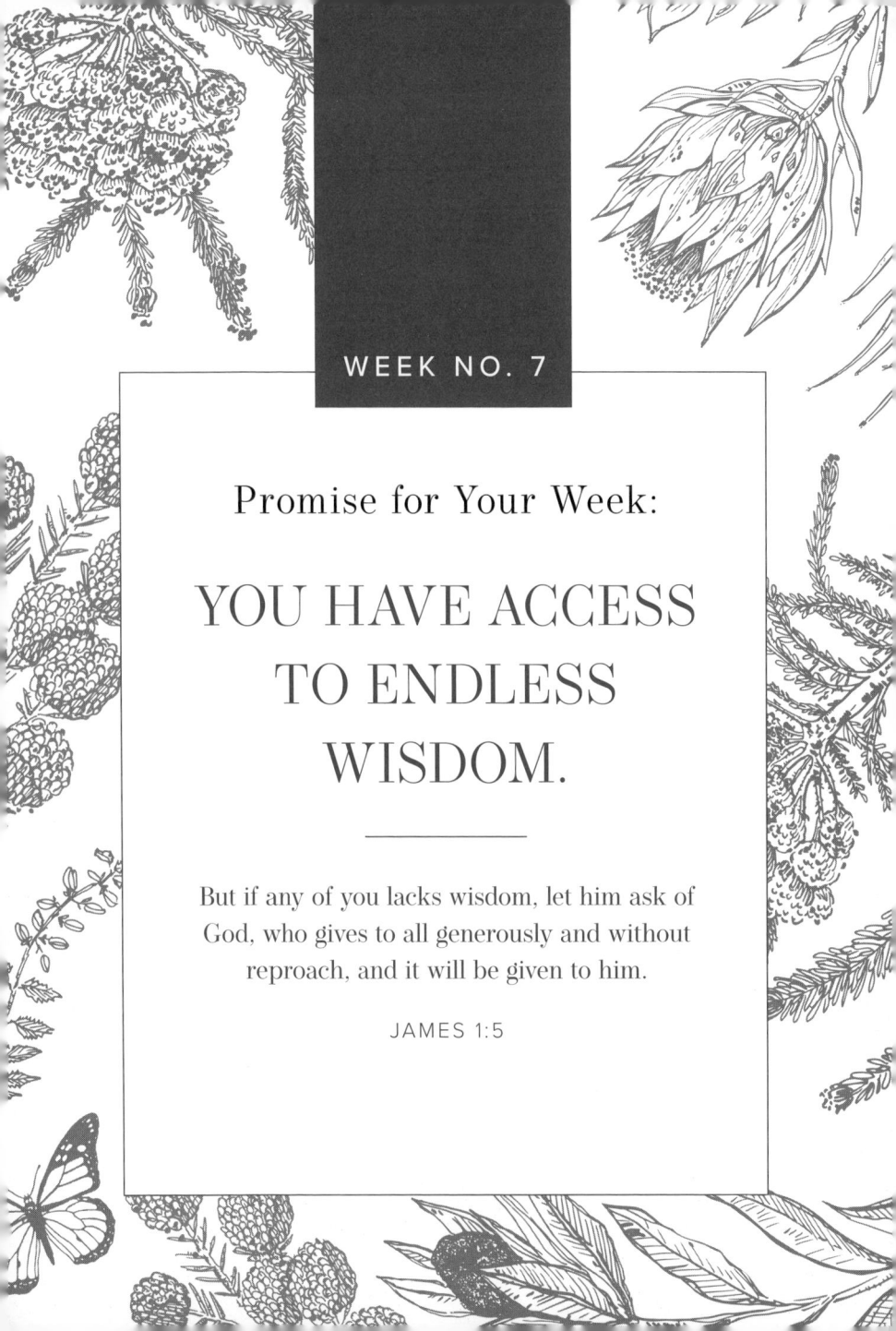

Promise for Your Week:

YOU HAVE ACCESS TO ENDLESS WISDOM.

But if any of you lacks wisdom, let him ask of God, who gives to all generously and without reproach, and it will be given to him.

JAMES 1:5

DAY 31

PLOT

After I handed over my Miss Universe title, I signed with a big modeling agency. My plan was to give the modeling world a shot, so I stayed in New York City for a second year. Many former Miss Universes take the modeling or acting route when their reign is over. So I considered it the expected route.

I'll never forget walking into one of my first casting calls. Actually, what I remember most was walking *out* of the room. My heart was heavy. The opportunity was a lucrative one. It likely would have set me up for a successful modeling career. But something didn't sit right in my spirit. The job would have required compromising my nonnegotiables as a Jesus follower. I wouldn't be required to do something unethical or illegal, but saying yes to the opportunity would have demanded representing myself in a way that wasn't God-honoring. The job didn't align with who I was or who I wanted to be. When I left the call, I knew I had made the right decision.

As young women striving to find our places in this complex world, we often face decisions that can alter the course of our lives. Where should we study? What career path should we choose? How do we handle relationships and all the things that come with being an adult?

As we try to answer these complicated questions, social media floods us with curated success stories. These seemingly perfect lives can distort our perception of what God wants for us. We can get overwhelmed by a sense of urgency and a fear of missing out, which can cloud our judgment and cause us to rush into decisions without seeking God's guidance.

Making the right choices is about more than what we decide to do in the moment; it is about deepening our relationship with God. The good news is that we are not alone in this process. God is with us every step of the way. And He gives us an endless supply of wisdom to help us choose the best for our lives. Let's explore how we can tap into this endless resource.

PRAYER FOR YOUR DAY

Heavenly Father, grant me clarity and wisdom in the situations I face each day. Guide my steps in Your truth as I strive to do the right thing. Strengthen my trust in Your perfect plan. In Jesus' name, amen.

YOU HAVE ACCESS TO ENDLESS WISDOM.

DAY 32

DIG

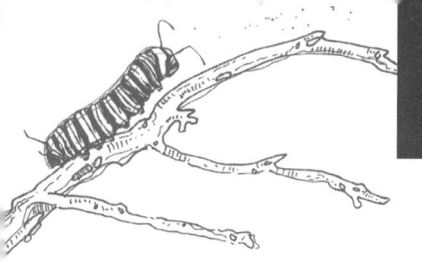

The survey below is intended to help you reflect on the ways you seek wisdom and make decisions in your daily life. Be transparent as you examine yourself.

How You Seek Wisdom

Read the statements below and indicate your level of agreement using numbers 1 through 5:

(1 = Strongly Disagree and 5 = Strongly Agree)

1. I frequently pray and seek God's guidance when I need to make important decisions. _____
2. The Bible is my go-to resource for understanding and direction in times of uncertainty. _____
3. I value the advice of my church leaders and spiritual mentors when facing difficult choices. _____
4. Reflective practices, such as journaling or meditative prayer, play a crucial role in my decision-making process. _____
5. Discussions with family and Christian friends help me discern the right path and make wise choices. _____

Total: _____

Self-Check Guide

5 to 10 points: Seed of potential. Do you feel like you're in the early stages of weaving faith into your decision-making? Let's dive deeper together and see how our faith can be watered in our daily choices this week.

11 to 15 points: Faith explorer. Do you use spiritual resources to guide you here and there? Like having a GPS that you use as a backup? Let's enable the turn-by-turn directions to navigate even more of life's tricky decisions.

16 to 20 points: Spiritual go-getter. It seems like you are leaning on your spiritual tool kit when making decisions, but there's always room to grow. How can we crank up the volume of our trust even more this week?

21 to 25 points: Decision crusher. Does your decision-making process feel like a vibrant mix of personal growth, wisdom from Scripture, and insights from your faith community? Isn't it great to have a spiritual toolbox with a variety of resources that help you make more God-honoring decisions?

A PRAYER FOR YOU FROM ME

Heavenly Father, please illuminate areas where this reader needs growth. Guide her decisions, give her wisdom, and deepen her faith as she walks with You. In Jesus' name, amen.

YOU HAVE ACCESS TO ENDLESS WISDOM.

DAY 33

PLANT

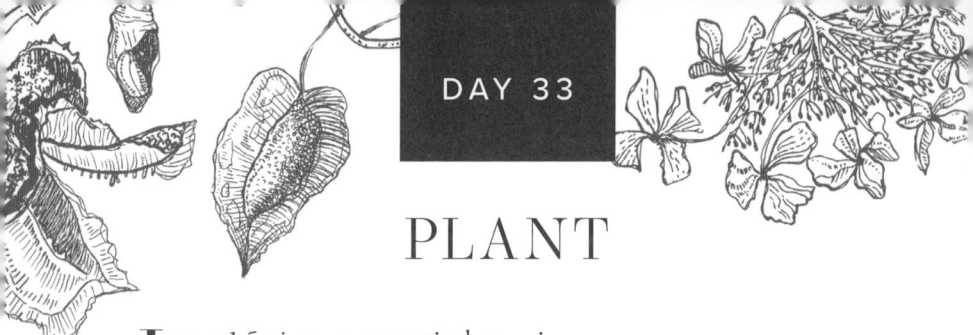

James 1:5 gives us a practical promise:

> But if any of you lacks wisdom, let him ask of God, who gives to all generously and without reproach, and it will be given to him.

This is so encouraging! I know I need God's wisdom in every decision I make. Having prayed for it when I was seeking a new career path after my Miss Universe era, I was guided by His prompting to say no to the opportunity I wrote about in this week's opening devotion.

When we seek God's wisdom, He generously opens our eyes to see and understand more than we could on our own. And let's be honest: We are all, on some level, wisdom-deficient. It doesn't matter how educated, wise, or filled with real-world experience we may be, we don't know the future. We don't know how certain decisions we make today will impact us for a lifetime. We need wisdom to see life through God's perspective and apply that to our lives.

What exactly is wisdom? Think of it as the life hack that helps you make the right choices, the kind that leads to better thoughts and actions. I have found that wisdom often steers me away from immediate gratification and toward greater joy.

What about the phrase "without reproach" in this week's verse? It means that when someone asks God for wisdom, God provides it freely and does not blame or scold the person for their lack of wisdom or for their previous mistakes. It emphasizes God's willingness to help and His open-hearted generosity in giving what is asked for, without making the person feel judged or inadequate. What a promise of divine provision!

Our Creator isn't just spinning galaxies; He also has a storehouse of wisdom ready to share. This is true in any situation, whether you're deciding on a college major, deciding between two jobs, or deciding about the relationship you're in.

Today come before God with an open heart, ready and willing to trust in His promise to give you wisdom whenever you need it.

PRAYER FOR YOUR DAY

Dear Lord, not only do I need You every day, but I need Your wisdom! Give me the courage to ask for it freely, knowing You are generous and will give it to me without reproach. In Jesus' name, amen.

YOU HAVE ACCESS TO ENDLESS WISDOM.

DAY 34

GROW

I love the passion that undergirds the words in Proverbs 2:2–5:

> Make your ear attentive to wisdom; incline your heart to understanding. For if you cry out for insight, and raise your voice for understanding; if you seek her as silver and search for her as for hidden treasures; then you will understand the fear of the LORD, and discover the knowledge of God.

Read out loud the following phrases:

- make your ear attentive
- incline your heart
- cry out for insight
- raise your voice for understanding
- search for [wisdom] as for hidden treasures

To me, this doesn't sound like a one-and-done prayer that's only spoken in desperate times; it's more like a lifelong walk in wisdom. We don't just wait until a certain critical moment arises in which we beg for wisdom (although God will freely give wisdom then too!); we proactively seek wisdom daily.

The habit of asking for wisdom each morning is essential to building my faith. I believe that doing so allowed my heart to hear and follow

God's prompting when the modeling opportunity wasn't the best for me. And God can do the same for you as you seek Him!

The best place to find wisdom is in His Word. When you read the Bible on a consistent basis, you are feeding your faith and tuning in to the Father's heart. His Word will lead and guide you in everything you do.

God's gift of wisdom doesn't guarantee that every answer will be immediately clear or that outcomes will always be expected. But God does promise that He will guide us, generously and without reservation, as we decide which path to follow.

Remember, wisdom is as valuable as a hidden treasure. Just ask! And keep asking. God will not hold back.

PRAYER FOR YOUR DAY

God, make my ears attentive to wisdom and incline my heart to understanding. I want to seek Your wisdom, knowing that it will guide me rightly. I'm so grateful for this amazing gift. Continue to teach me how to trust in You. In Jesus' name, amen.

> **YOU HAVE ACCESS TO ENDLESS WISDOM.**

DAY 35

FLOURISH

Today let's read, meditate on, and memorize James 1:5

When seeking God's wisdom, we should surround ourselves with people who regularly seek God's wisdom. When I turned down that modeling opportunity, I was surrounded by a faith-filled community—my fiancé, friends, and my family—all praying for God's best in my life. Because these people shared my values, their support made the decision to say no a bit easier.

Proverbs 13:20 says, "One who walks with wise people will be wise, but a companion of fools will suffer harm." Spend a few minutes reflecting on this verse and how it applies to your journey in seeking wisdom through your relationships. Think of the five people you spend the most time with. Note how they influence your faith and decision-making. How does each relationship contribute to your spiritual growth? Do they encourage you to seek wisdom and live according to God's Word?

Remember, surrounding yourself with godly wisdom is an ongoing process that requires intentional choices and prayerful consideration.

PRAYER FOR YOUR DAY

Lord, give me the wisdom to put You first in my decisions. I ask You to surround me with people who will encourage me to put You first in my life and love and serve others. In Jesus' name, amen.

YOU HAVE ACCESS TO ENDLESS WISDOM.

WEEK NO. 8

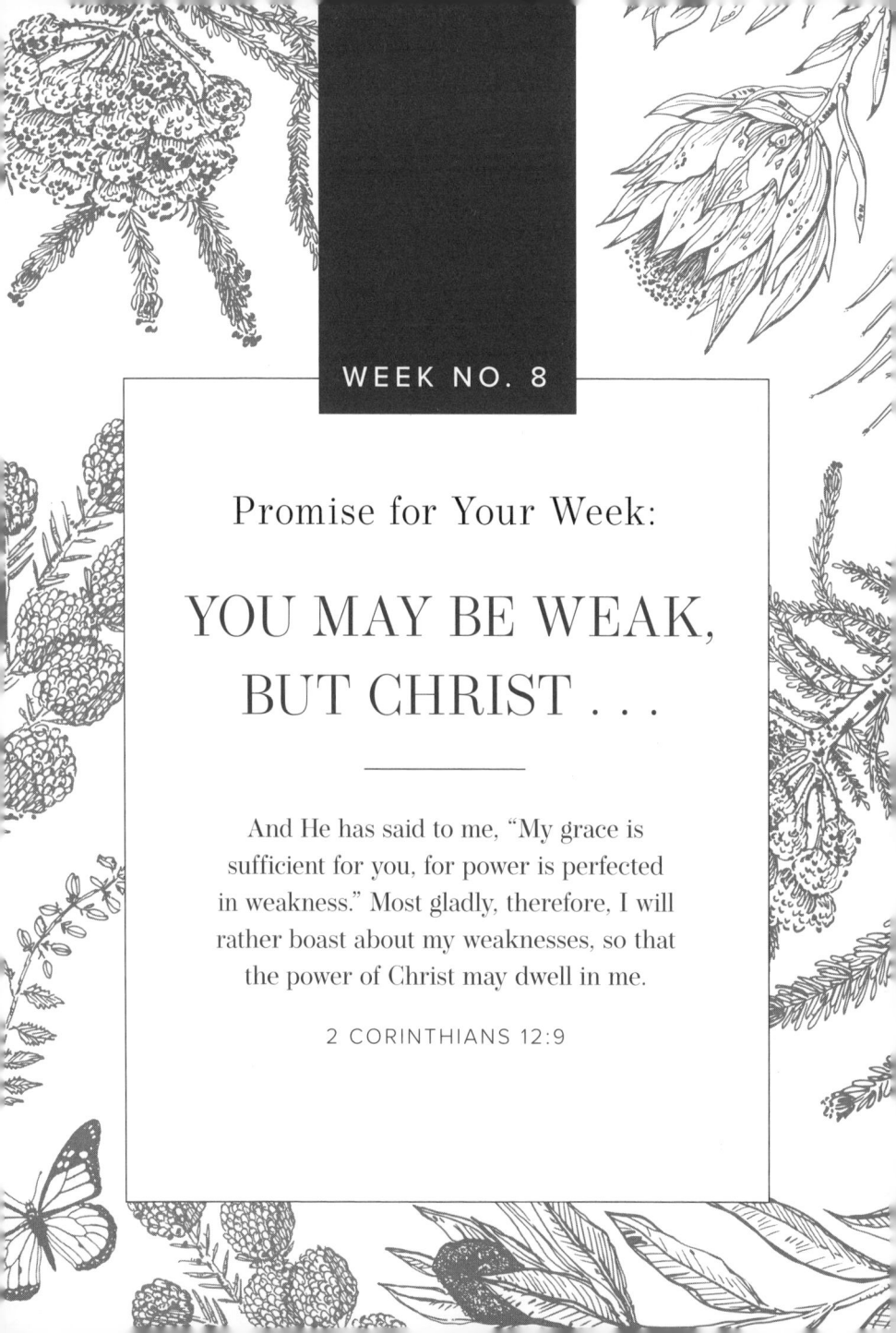

Promise for Your Week:

YOU MAY BE WEAK, BUT CHRIST . . .

And He has said to me, "My grace is sufficient for you, for power is perfected in weakness." Most gladly, therefore, I will rather boast about my weaknesses, so that the power of Christ may dwell in me.

2 CORINTHIANS 12:9

DAY 36

PLOT

I can't sing to save my life, and I have my sister to thank for making me aware of it. I was eleven when Franje was born. She was the cutest baby I'd ever seen. I'll never forget holding her for the first time. Her skin felt like a rose petal and smelled just as sweet. As I cuddled my baby sister in my arms, inhaling her baby scent, outlining her silky-smooth face with my fingers, and staring into the most beautiful green-gray eyes I have ever seen, I started to softly sing a lullaby. All I could think of was how my dreams had come true: One day this little girl and I would dress up in fancy clothes and have tea parties, and I'd teach her how to play field hockey. I knew everything would be just perfect. It was a tender moment—one that wouldn't last.

The minute my voice poured out the first notes of a random lullaby, Franje burst into tears. Full-blown screams, as if I'd just dipped her tiny hand in ice water. While my baby sister wailed, I froze. What had I done wrong? But I realized it was the singing, because the second I stopped, Franje stopped crying. She may have even smiled. It was a special bonding moment for us, *despite* my imperfect voice.

While this may be a silly example, it helps paint the picture that we all have weaknesses—*singing* being one of mine (which, to be honest, hasn't gotten much better!). I may not know what your weaknesses are, but I do know that your weakness does not define how Jesus sees you—just like my singing did not define my relationship with Franje. My vocal shortcomings did not affect her love for me nor my love for and commitment to her.

Maybe you can sing like Mariah Carey, but you were born with dyslexia, like my husband. Perhaps you have a disability, like cerebral palsy, or maybe you are struggling with addiction, and it feels like there's no way out, leaving you questioning how God could ever use you in His greater plan.

Guess what? These weaknesses open the door for God to shine the brightest—not because of our own talents but through His perfect grace and power at work in and through imperfect people.

In a world that constantly pushes us toward perfection, it can be overwhelming to address our limitations. Yet, in our weaknesses, we can vividly see the grace of God at work because the King of creation sees those shortcomings as clearly as we do and still wants to be our friend who sticks closer than a sister.

PRAYER FOR YOUR DAY

God, remind me that I'm Your instrument, perfectly imperfect and still making a difference. I don't have to be flawless to reflect Your love. Help me embrace my weaknesses, trusting that You'll turn them into something amazing. In Jesus' name, amen.

YOU MAY BE WEAK, BUT CHRIST . . .

DAY 37

DIG

Today you'll complete a writing exercise that will help you to articulate and offer your weaknesses and insecurities to God, transforming how you perceive them in the light of His grace.

1. **Prepare your space.** Find a quiet, comfortable spot where you can reflect without interruptions and distractions. Set the tone by lighting a candle or putting on soft worship music.
2. **Pray for openness.** Ask God to open your heart and guide your words as you write.
3. **Start writing your letter.** Reflect on the areas where you feel you fall short. These could be traits you wish you didn't have, skills you lack, or areas where you frequently feel inadequate or overwhelmed.

    Consider how these particular weaknesses and insecurities affect you. How do they make you feel about yourself? How do they impact your day-to-day life and your relationships?

    Write about how you hope God will use these weaknesses for good. Ask for His perspective on them and how they might be used to fulfill His purposes.
4. **Express trust.** Conclude by affirming your trust in God's plan and timing. Acknowledge that while you may not understand why you struggle with these issues, you believe He is at work in every aspect of your life.

After finishing your letter, spend a few minutes in silence reflecting on what you've written. Consider any new insights or feelings that emerged during this exercise. Plan to revisit it in a few months to see how your feelings and perspectives might have changed or how God might have worked through your acknowledged weaknesses. You are well on your way to seeing how God transforms our vulnerabilities into strengths and how our deepest insecurities can reveal His greatest work in our lives.

_____

_____

_____

_____

_____

A PRAYER FOR YOU FROM ME

God, thank You that we can come to You for anything and be our true selves. You will always love and accept us without condition. I pray for the reader who is writing this letter. Help her to express herself without fear and without holding back. May she trust in Your power to transform her weaknesses into Your strength. In Jesus' name, amen.

YOU MAY BE WEAK, BUT CHRIST . . .

DAY 38

PLANT

In 2 Corinthians 12, we delve into a more personal aspect of the apostle Paul's life. He described a metaphorical "thorn in the flesh" (v. 7), a phrase that encapsulates a constant, excruciating affliction that plagued him. Despite his begging God three times to remove this torment, it persisted. Scholars have suggested that this thorn was likely a long-term affliction. They have proposed several possible explanations for what this thorn was: Paul could have struggled with anxiety, challenges in his ministry, or a physical malady. Ultimately, we don't know what the thorn was. Scripture's intent is not to uncover Paul's specific struggle but to expose its purpose.

While God didn't take Paul's thorn away, He did give the missionary something else. Something deeper. Something better. Paul wrote:

> And He [God] has said to me, "My grace is sufficient for you, for power is perfected in weakness." Most gladly, therefore, I will rather boast about my weaknesses, so that the power of Christ may dwell in me. (2 Corinthians 12:9)

Paul's struggle was an invitation to welcome God's power to display divine strength in human frailty. This idea is mind-blowing. Weakness and strength are opposites. One doesn't have much to do with the other. But here God is saying that weakness brings about strength. Like many other biblical principles, this promise is a paradox.

When God told Paul that His power was perfected in Paul's weakness, it unlocked a new perspective on his struggle. He even began to boast about this shortcoming!

There's no question about it: Thorns suck. Most of us don't want to accept hard things as something good. Especially when there are a lot of gut-wrenching thorns that supersede the simple annoyance of not being able to sing or do something well. But if we can take on Paul's perspective, we can exchange our weakness for God's strength. Are you able to see your thorns not as obstacles or insufferable situations but as sacred spaces where God's power can unfold?

The strength of Christ to fill in the gap of my weakness? Yes, please!

PRAYER FOR YOUR DAY

Lord, while I long to be free of my weaknesses, I trust in Your perfect wisdom. Thank You for using these challenges as opportunities for love, compassion, and drawing me closer to You. Help me to courageously accept my weaknesses and engage with Your wonderful plans for me. In Jesus' name, amen.

YOU MAY BE WEAK, BUT CHRIST . . .

DAY 39

GROW

When are you reminded of your frailties and flaws? Is it when you compare yourself or your life to others? Most of us fall prey to the trap of comparison. Our spirits often sag when we observe other women who seemingly have it all—and have it all together. Well, there's good news. It's right there, in the moment you feel the furthest from being the strong and confident woman God created you to be, that God whispers a perfect promise in your heart: His power is made perfect in your weakness.

Now that you know this truth, let's explore three ways of letting God's strength shine through your faults, inadequacies, or pain.

1. **Embrace your imperfections.** In a culture that often tells us to hide our struggles behind a filter of perfection, admitting we're anything less than fine can seem daunting. But there is sacred beauty and freedom in being real with God about where we need Him most. Whether you're wrestling with insecurity, decision paralysis, or a heartache that just won't heal, bring it to Him. It's the first step in moving from your strength to His.
2. **Share in the safety of community.** God didn't design us to walk through life alone. One of the most beautiful aspects of our faith is community—those God-given friendships that build us up and remind us that we aren't alone in our struggles. When we open up about our weaknesses, we're not

only unburdening ourselves; we're giving others permission to do the same. This vulnerability creates a space for God's power to work not just in us, but through us.
3. **Depend daily on God.** Let's start each day not by picking up our phones or tackling our to-do list but with a prayer that places our weaknesses into God's hands and asks for His strength to be evident. This daily surrender is powerful. It shifts our focus from what we can do to what God can do.

Embracing our weaknesses allows us to experience God's power in a way that isn't possible when we're busy pretending everything is perfect. Like Paul, we can then joyfully boast in our weaknesses because they highlight Christ's infinite capacity to work through us.

PRAYER FOR YOUR DAY

Dear Lord, help me to surrender my weaknesses daily, seeing them not as setbacks but as setups for Your mighty power to work within me. Teach me to trust in Your perfect strength. In Jesus' name, amen.

YOU MAY BE WEAK, BUT CHRIST . . .

DAY 40

FLOURISH

Today let's read, meditate on, and memorize 2 Corinthians 12:9. Every time you feel inadequate or unqualified, remember you're invited to the same transformation Paul experienced when he saw God's power at work. Paul embraced his weaknesses for Christ's strength to shine, and I challenge you to do the same.

1. Take a moment to reflect on the insecurities/weaknesses you listed earlier this week.
2. Read 2 Corinthians 12:9 out loud and slowly three times. Each time, focus on a different aspect of the verse: God's grace, the perfection of His power, and the presence of weaknesses.
3. Consider why you are grateful for each weakness/insecurity. How might it be a setup for experiencing God's power? (For example, your anxiety might teach you to depend deeply on God's peace.)
4. Pray for each weakness. Ask God to help you see them as opportunities to display His strength. Ask that each weakness become a source of joy as you boast in God's good work.

PRAYER FOR YOUR DAY

Lord, help me to trust You with my imperfections. Use them to make Your name known, Lord. In Jesus' name, amen.

YOU MAY BE WEAK, BUT CHRIST . . .

WEEK NO. 9

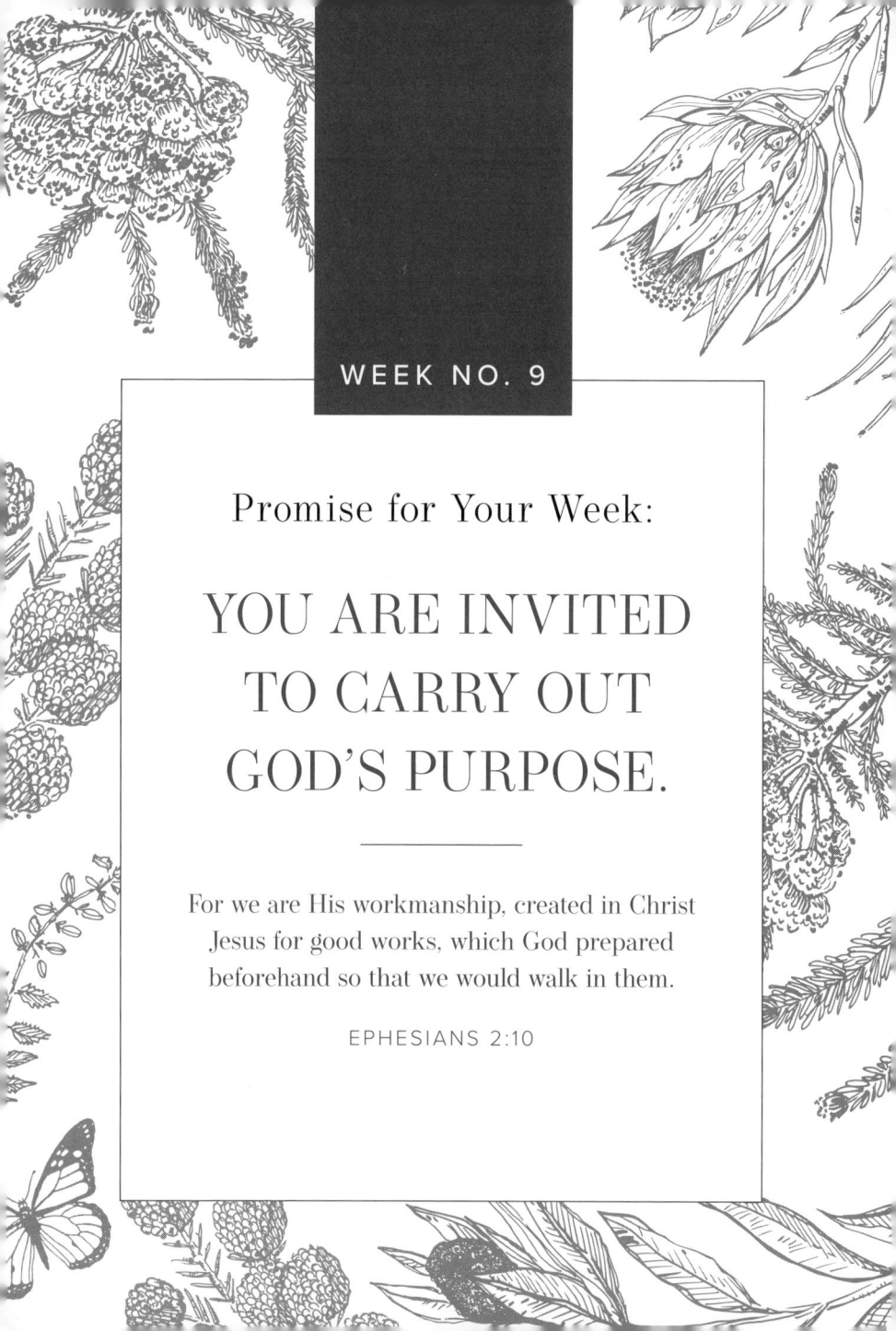

Promise for Your Week:

YOU ARE INVITED TO CARRY OUT GOD'S PURPOSE.

For we are His workmanship, created in Christ Jesus for good works, which God prepared beforehand so that we would walk in them.

EPHESIANS 2:10

DAY 41

PLOT

When Tim and I first met, we seemed to have very little in common. I was a pageant queen and an ambassador for South Africa. He was an American football player, which I could appreciate but didn't know much about at the time.

Even our first languages had their differences. My native language is Afrikaans, which can sound harsh and aggressive, a bit like German. One of the first times Tim heard me speak it was when I was talking with my mom, who lives in South Africa, over the phone. After I hung up, he asked me with a concerned look on his face, "Why are you guys fighting?" I couldn't help but laugh. "We weren't fighting," I replied. "I was talking to her about the dogs!"

There were so many things for us to learn about each other—culture, language, family, interests, and more. But building relationships is about more than sharing a love for sports or having the same taste in music or food. When Tim and I met, we shared something significant: purpose. I have a heart for the fight against human trafficking and a deep love for the special-needs community because of my sister, Franje. Tim has a heart for people who are in their deepest, darkest hour of need, people the world often overlooks—people just like my little sister. We were united not by preferences that can change but by an underlying purpose: to fight for those who can't fight for themselves.

Purpose is one of those words that has many meanings. Society pushes us toward defining our life's purpose in terms of career milestones, financial prosperity, or social status. Even church circles use it haphazardly or without thought. But for those of us who follow Christ, the concept of purpose is not about worldly accolades. Simply put, as children of God, our purpose is to love and serve Him and others (Matthew 22:37–40).

Living out this true purpose doesn't necessarily mean abandoning personal goals or career aspirations. Instead, we can infuse our everyday tasks and responsibilities with love and service. Whether you are a student, a professional, or a parent, everything you do can reflect God's love. When we approach each day with this kind of God-given purpose, we can tap into eternity. We do things that have a lasting impact instead of focusing on self-gratification. What we choose to do today can bring meaning to tomorrow.

PRAYER FOR YOUR DAY

God, as the days seem shorter and busier, guide my attention toward the universal purpose that You have called me to. Help me to live purposefully, loving and serving You and others, reflecting Your grace in all I do. In Jesus' name, amen.

YOU ARE INVITED TO CARRY OUT GOD'S PURPOSE.

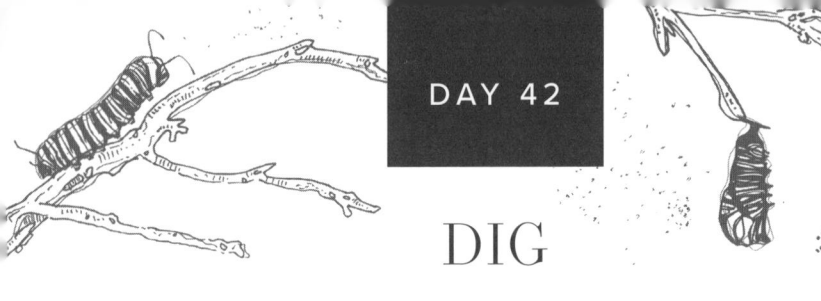

DAY 42

DIG

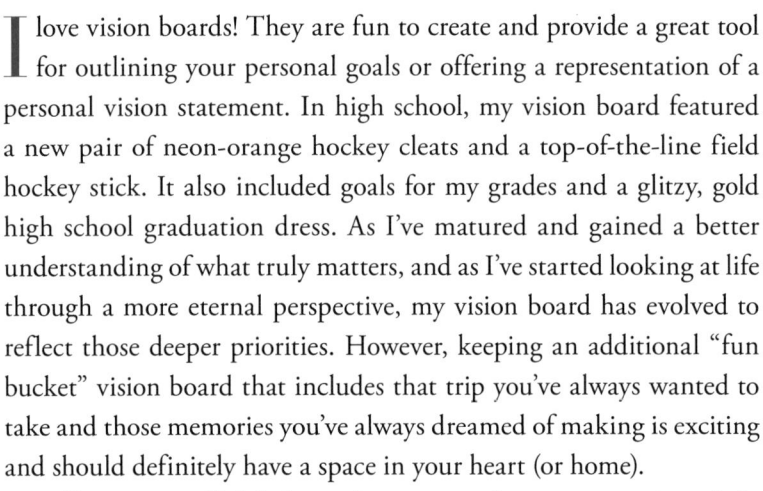

I love vision boards! They are fun to create and provide a great tool for outlining your personal goals or offering a representation of a personal vision statement. In high school, my vision board featured a new pair of neon-orange hockey cleats and a top-of-the-line field hockey stick. It also included goals for my grades and a glitzy, gold high school graduation dress. As I've matured and gained a better understanding of what truly matters, and as I've started looking at life through a more eternal perspective, my vision board has evolved to reflect those deeper priorities. However, keeping an additional "fun bucket" vision board that includes that trip you've always wanted to take and those memories you've always dreamed of making is exciting and should definitely have a space in your heart (or home).

I'll start us off: I believe that a part of my purpose is to help women understand their true worth, discover their God-given purpose, and build a lasting confidence through my books, social media communities, conferences, and speaking opportunities. And so my vision board includes some of my hopes and dreams on how I plan to live out my purpose more intentionally every year.

Today it's your turn to show off your creative side and make a vision board that represents how you understand and feel about God's purpose for your life.

You can create a digital vision board (i.e., Canva.com) or a physical one with a corkboard or poster board. Add images, Bible verses, quotes, and anything else that inspires a purpose-filled you. Take your time and get creative. You don't have to finish the vision board before you move on to the next devotional, but whenever you are finished, put it in a place where you'll see it regularly.

Some ideas to get you thinking:

- What key verse speaks to you in this season?
- Do you have time, talents, or treasures that you want to steward differently?
- What areas of your life do you want to invest in more? Relationships, friendships, community, quiet time, etc.?
- Is there a specific area of your life where you want to serve others more?
- Is there anything that you've been significantly convicted about this season?

This activity is not just about planning the future but affirming God's role in your life and how you can live out His calling day by day. Feel free to update your vision board throughout the year.

A PRAYER FOR YOU FROM ME

God, I pray for the reader working on her vision board. Fill her with Your divine inspiration. Let each image and word reflect the profound purpose You have designed for her life. In Jesus' name, amen.

YOU ARE INVITED TO CARRY OUT GOD'S PURPOSE.

DAY 43

PLANT

One of the best examples of a person with purpose is the apostle Paul. Talk about someone who was committed to God's purpose for him and the church. He experienced setbacks, uncertain paths, and unimaginable persecution as he carried on about God's mission for the early church. In fact, he was likely in prison when he wrote to the church in Ephesus. One of my husband's favorite Bible verses, Ephesians 2:10, says:

> For we are His workmanship, created in Christ Jesus for good works, which God prepared beforehand so that we would walk in them.

The Greek word used for "workmanship" is etymologically related to the English word *poem*.[12] Some translations, such as the New International Version, fittingly substitute "handiwork" for "workmanship." This means we belong to God, each of us handcrafted by the ultimate Creator. As the saying goes, "God doesn't make mistakes!" Truly, we are His masterpieces, not because of what we've done but because of what God has done in us.

We are masterpieces solely because we are God's creation, owing nothing to our own efforts or merits. The Bible talks about our identity as God's workmanship in many beautiful ways. Here are just a few:

- We are made in the image of God (Genesis 1:27).
- We are awesomely and wonderfully made (Psalm 139:14).
- We are individually known by God (Matthew 10:30).

When Jesus sacrificed Himself on the cross, not only did He offer a perfect picture of divine love, but God was also composing the most profound love poem, the song of new creation through redemption. Christ's death allows us to transform from blank slates into awe-inspiring works of beauty.

You are His living poem! When you view yourself through this lens of sacred artistry, you can begin to understand the depth of your worth and the extent of His grace. Here's the thing about masterpieces: They take time to create. As you spend time with God, you grow and become more like Jesus. Every day presents a new opportunity to embrace your identity as God's handiwork.

Remember, you are unique—a one-of-a-kind masterpiece. There is absolutely no one else like you! Embrace this truth, knowing that every detail of your life has a magnificent design.

PRAYER FOR YOUR DAY

Dear Lord, Your Word tells me that because of Your Son's death on the cross and resurrection from the dead, I am a masterpiece. Help me to recognize my worth in You. Teach me to see myself as You do—precious and wonderfully made. In Jesus' name, amen.

YOU ARE INVITED TO CARRY OUT GOD'S PURPOSE.

DAY 44

GROW

For we are His workmanship, created in Christ Jesus for good works, which God prepared beforehand so that we would walk in them (Ephesians 2:10).

Understanding that we are "created in Christ Jesus for good works" reveals a purpose that transcends our routine ambitions. This isn't about what job we have, which school we attend, or our family tree. It's deeper; it's about the essence of who we are in Christ. We are crafted by God's own hands, and within us He has planted seeds of His divine purpose—good works that He has prepared in advance for us to do.

Imagine that: Before you took your first breath, God had a plan for your life. These plans are not random tasks; they are missions that fit into a much larger, divine puzzle. Each action, each decision you make, can align with God's magnificent plan, contributing to His kingdom in ways you might not immediately understand but nonetheless matter. Read the verses below and meditate on how you were created for a purpose:

- 2 Corinthians 5:20: "We are therefore Christ's ambassadors, as though God were making his appeal through us. We implore you on Christ's behalf: Be reconciled to God" (NIV). In the kingdom of God, we all have a responsibility to represent Jesus.
- Romans 12:4–5: "For just as we have many parts in one body and all the body's parts do not have the same function, so we, who are many, are one body in Christ, and individually parts

of one another." In the kingdom of God, we all have a role to play as we work together.
- Matthew 5:14–16: "You are the light of the world. A town built on a hill cannot be hidden. Neither do people light a lamp and put it under a bowl. Instead they put it on its stand, and it gives light to everyone in the house. In the same way, let your light shine before others, that they may see your good deeds and glorify your Father in heaven" (NIV). In the kingdom of God, we don't take the credit; we give the credit to the One who deserves it.

You are not an accident. God created you with the intention to influence the world in a special and lasting way. We are co-laborers with Christ, which means we work together with Him to do good works. Think of Ephesians 2:10 as a divine invitation to join God in making a difference in the lives of those around you. Instead of thinking of this as one assignment, consider each day another chance to be more like Jesus to others. Be kind. Show mercy. Pitch in when no one else does. Show love through acts of service. Each choice and each action then becomes a revelation of Christ's purposeful love flowing through you.

PRAYER FOR YOUR DAY

Heavenly Father, I ask You to reveal and unlock the good works You have prepared for me. Open my eyes and my heart to how I can fulfill Your purpose and serve Your kingdom faithfully. In Jesus' name, amen.

YOU ARE INVITED TO CARRY OUT GOD'S PURPOSE.

DAY 45

FLOURISH

Today let's read, meditate on, and memorize Ephesians 2:10.

Let's go back to your vision board I asked you to create a few days ago. I want you to add to it based on what you learned about the promise of the week: You are invited to carry out God's purpose.

Reflect on this promise below and include images on your vision board that remind you of the following truths:

- You are a masterpiece.
- You can choose joy knowing your worth in Christ.
- You were made on purpose for a purpose.
- You can partner with God to do good works.

Use this vision board as a daily reminder that you can make the right choices and decisions and use your time wisely to reflect God's redeeming work in your life.

PRAYER FOR YOUR DAY

Father God, You are the potter and I am the clay. May my life and purpose be formed in the way You want it. Give me a heart of obedience to trust and follow where You're leading me. I want my hands to be where You're working; my feet to be where You're going. May I fall more in love with Your kingdom come! In Jesus' name, amen.

YOU ARE INVITED TO CARRY OUT GOD'S PURPOSE.

WEEK NO. 10

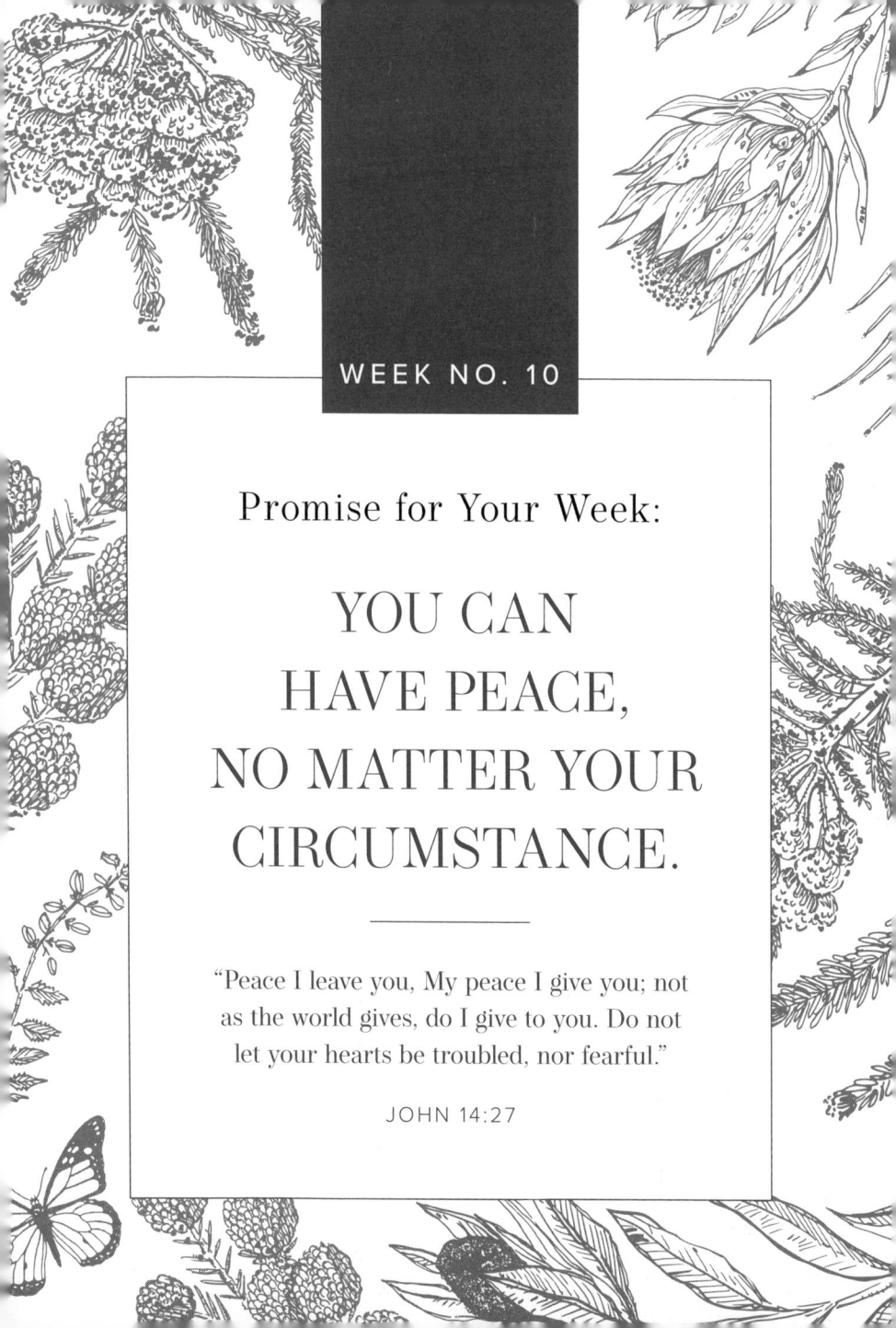

Promise for Your Week:

YOU CAN HAVE PEACE, NO MATTER YOUR CIRCUMSTANCE.

"Peace I leave you, My peace I give you; not as the world gives, do I give to you. Do not let your hearts be troubled, nor fearful."

JOHN 14:27

DAY 46

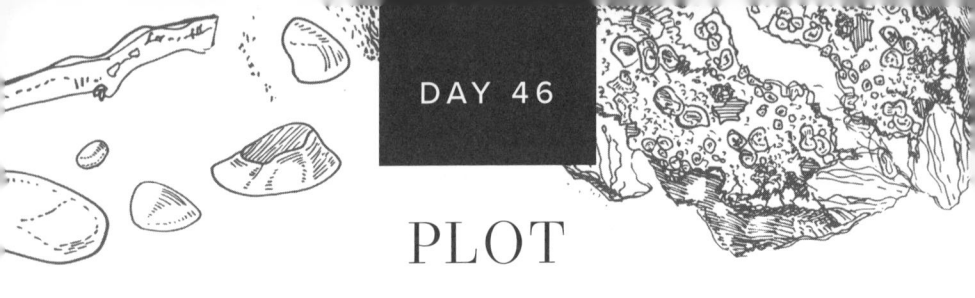

PLOT

On May 4, 2019, shortly after her thirteenth birthday, the most significant earthly motivator in my life left earth to go be with Jesus. Franje, my little sister and the daughter of my dad and stepmom, was born with a brain dysgenesis, which means that the normal development of the white and gray matter of the brain had been disrupted. The result was threefold: a subtotal cerebellar agenesis, an underdeveloped corpus callosum and brain stem, as well as microcephaly.[13] In simpler terms, the cerebellum is one of three parts of the brain, and while small, it's pretty important. The cerebellum is responsible for brain functions like language processing, memory, and muscle control,[14] which helps you to eat, drive, scratch an itch, brush your teeth, walk—all things Franje was unable to do on her own.

Franje's slow progress was a challenge, but each small step forward was celebrated. With physical therapy and neurological programs, we saw hope! At one year old, Franje made movements resembling crawling and showed excitement recognizing voices. Though we accepted she might not reach typical milestones, these signs offered hope for greater independence. Unfortunately, she later developed West syndrome, also known as infantile spasms syndrome. Hope faded as it erased all her hard-earned progress. She survived but never recuperated and remained functioning at a three-month-old level thereafter.

I had my first faith crisis when she was diagnosed. I didn't understand why my innocent sister had to be born with such a devastating illness. Why did she have to suffer physically? What had she done to deserve not being able to talk or walk or swim? What was God thinking when He created her, knowing she would never get to go to school, play sports, or walk down the aisle one day to marry the love of her life? Over time, I learned that even without answers or a miraculous recovery for Franje, Jesus was the giver of peace. It was up to me to accept the gift.

Our lives often feel like we are riding a roller coaster blindfolded. One minute we're up, celebrating achievements, love, and those rare moments of perfect Instagram selfies. The next we're plummeting into the depths of "What on earth am I doing with my life?," exams that will determine our futures, chronic illnesses that leave us begging for relief, and the never-ending pressure to figure it all out.

These challenges, along with pursuing a life that's pleasing to God, can make peace feel like a distant, unattainable concept. If you're anything like me, you know it's hard to feel peace in the world. It's not something that comes naturally, especially when we find ourselves in circumstances outside of our control.

This week we'll explore how to receive peace, even when our worlds are falling apart.

PRAYER FOR YOUR DAY

Lord, thank You for not calling me to live in this world absent of Your presence. You have come to this earth to set me free and to show that You are bigger than anything we face in this life. Remind me that peace—Your peace—is possible even in pandemonium. In Jesus' name, amen.

> **YOU CAN HAVE PEACE, NO MATTER YOUR CIRCUMSTANCE.**

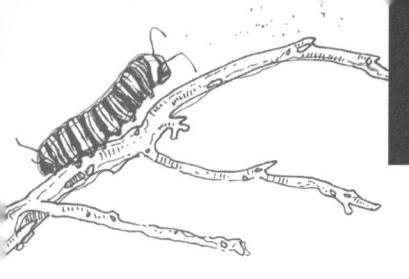

DAY 47

DIG

In the midst of the daily hustle, where do you find your peace? Today let's identify whether you're tapping into God's deep, steadfast peace or the fleeting peace the world offers. Only you know what your relationship with God is like. This exercise is simply an opportunity to reflect on your past week and assess what you run to for peace.

Where You Find Your Peace

Read the statements below and indicate your level of agreement using numbers 1 to 5:

(1 = Strongly Disagree and 5 = Strongly Agree)

1. When I face uncertainty, it's hard for me to turn to prayer or Scripture. _____
2. I often find myself scrolling through social media or seeking friends' advice when I feel anxious or stressed. _____
3. I often rely on distractions like binge-watching TV, shopping, or eating to ease my worries. _____
4. I tend to feel more at peace after achieving personal goals or receiving praise and recognition. _____
5. I feel that peace is most attainable when I control every aspect of my life. _____

Total: _____

If you found it tricky to judge yourself, you are not alone! Jeremiah 17:9 says, "The human mind is more deceitful than anything else" (NET). I'm proud of you for taking the time to answer honestly!

Self-Check Guide

5 to 10 Points: You go, girl! Let's keep deepening your spiritual roots.

11 to 15 Points: You might experience a mix of sometimes leaning on God's peace and other times being distracted by the world. Let's find new ways to run to God consistently.

16 to 20 Points: You might often seek the world's peace to navigate life's storms. Is there anything you'd like to do to tap into the deep peace God offers? Give it a try this week.

21 to 25 Points: You might feel like the sources you normally run to for peace sustain you well. Let's learn some new ways this week.

A PRAYER FOR YOU FROM ME

Dear Lord, help this reader to find serenity in You alone, amid life's storms. Reveal to her ways that she can tap into Your eternal peace over fleeting worldly comforts. In Jesus' name, amen.

YOU CAN HAVE PEACE, NO MATTER YOUR CIRCUMSTANCE.

DAY 48

PLANT

A few times in Scripture, Jesus found Himself on a boat with His disciples in stormy seas. In each instance, the disciples were frightened that the boat would capsize and they would drown, whereas Jesus was the picture of calm, cool, and collected. He even slept through one of the storms! I suppose, with His being the actual Prince of Peace, serenity came naturally to Him. But let's not forget that Jesus was fully God and fully human, and serenity does not come naturally to us humans. Amid the wild ride of life, which often robs our peace, Jesus is our best example and offers a promise found in John 14:27:

> Peace I leave you, My peace I give you; not as the world gives, do I give to you. Do not let your hearts be troubled, nor fearful.

This isn't your run-of-the-mill, take-a-spa-day/nap/time off kind of peace. It's a deep "even though the world is a hot mess, I'm gonna be okay" kind of peace. This peace that Jesus offers is not dependent on circumstances, how many likes we get, or whether we've figured out our life's plan by twenty, thirty, or even fifty.

Think about it. Have you ever had a moment where everything felt right, even though things around you were far from perfect? Maybe it was a quiet morning with a cup of coffee before the world woke up or that feeling you get when your favorite song comes on and you can't help but dance. That's a glimpse of the peace Jesus is talking about.

This peace changes how we live. When you're rooted in peace, you can face the chaos of life without being shaken. It's like being in the eye of the storm, where everything around you is whirling but you're standing firm. So the next time you're scrolling through social media feeling like everyone else has it together, or you're wondering if your dreams will ever take off, or you're reeling from confusion and anger because a loved one got diagnosed with a terminal illness, take a deep breath. Remind yourself of Jesus' promise. His peace is not a fluffy, feel-good idea; it's a power-packed promise that holds true, no matter what.

Remember: God's gift of peace will hold you together when things around you are falling apart.

PRAYER FOR YOUR DAY

Dear Lord, knowing I am unable to control everything, I give it all to You. I am thankful for blessings, forgiveness, and even trials. I believe in Your peace. It's the peace I seek. In Jesus' name, amen.

> **YOU CAN HAVE PEACE, NO MATTER YOUR CIRCUMSTANCE.**

DAY 49

GROW

Peace is in our possession. Jesus has gifted it to each one of us. The million-dollar question is, how do we live in that peace? This is an important question because peace isn't like magic dust we sprinkle over ourselves as needed. Yes, peace may be a gift, but it does require something of us. We must learn how to practice peace.

Here are a few keys to accessing the power of this gift:

- **Peace in His presence:** Flood your mind with the life-changing truths of Scripture. Think of Psalm 119:165 as your spiritual superpower: "Those who love Your Law have great peace, and nothing causes them to stumble."
- **Forgiveness is freedom:** Kick bitterness and grudges to the curb. Drop the heavy stuff and forgive, just like Jesus did for you.
- **Gratitude is the attitude:** Make thankfulness your demeanor. First Thessalonians 5:18 says to be grateful in all things because that's the key to living in God's will and finding joy in the everyday.
- **Relationship goals:** Aim for peace and understanding in all your relationships. Romans 12:18 is your reminder that living in harmony isn't just a good idea; it's a God idea: "If possible, so far as it depends on you, be at peace with all people."
- **Self-control strategies:** Let the Holy Spirit be your coach in the gym of self-discipline. Galatians 5:22–23 shows us that

self-control isn't about restriction; it's about living freely and fully in God's peace.

When you are wavering in chaos or crisis, remember that you are held and adored by the One who calms seas and quiets storms. Dive deep into the peace of God. Let it settle in your heart and watch how it transforms not just your mindset but your life.

PRAYER FOR YOUR DAY

Heavenly Father, guide me to cultivate Your peace in my heart. It's so hard sometimes! Teach me to accept, nurture, and spread the gift of peace through faith, love, and daily surrender to Your will. In Jesus' name, amen.

> **YOU CAN HAVE PEACE, NO MATTER YOUR CIRCUMSTANCE.**

DAY 50

FLOURISH

Today let's read, meditate on, and memorize John 14:27.

I want to close this week by reminding you that God is your provider. When you seek His kingdom first, as Matthew 6:31–33 tells us, He will give you everything you need. It may not be according to your preferences or timelines, but one thing is certain: God is faithful.

Although I tend to use the NASB or NIV translation of Scripture, sometimes I love reading a verse in different translations. It can help me see the verse in a new light. Open a Bible app and read John 14:27 in different translations like the NLT, Amplified, or The Living Bible. Write your favorite version below.

Remember, inner peace doesn't come from what is happening around us; it comes from who is within us.

PRAYER FOR YOUR DAY

Father, thank You for allowing me to have such free access to Your Word. Please speak to me as I open Your Word to find peace. Embrace me in Your love and wisdom. Guide me in my planning and actions. Teach me how You work so that I can follow in Your ways. Bless me and have grace with me as I take these steps toward You, Lord. Amen.

YOU CAN HAVE PEACE, NO MATTER YOUR CIRCUMSTANCE.

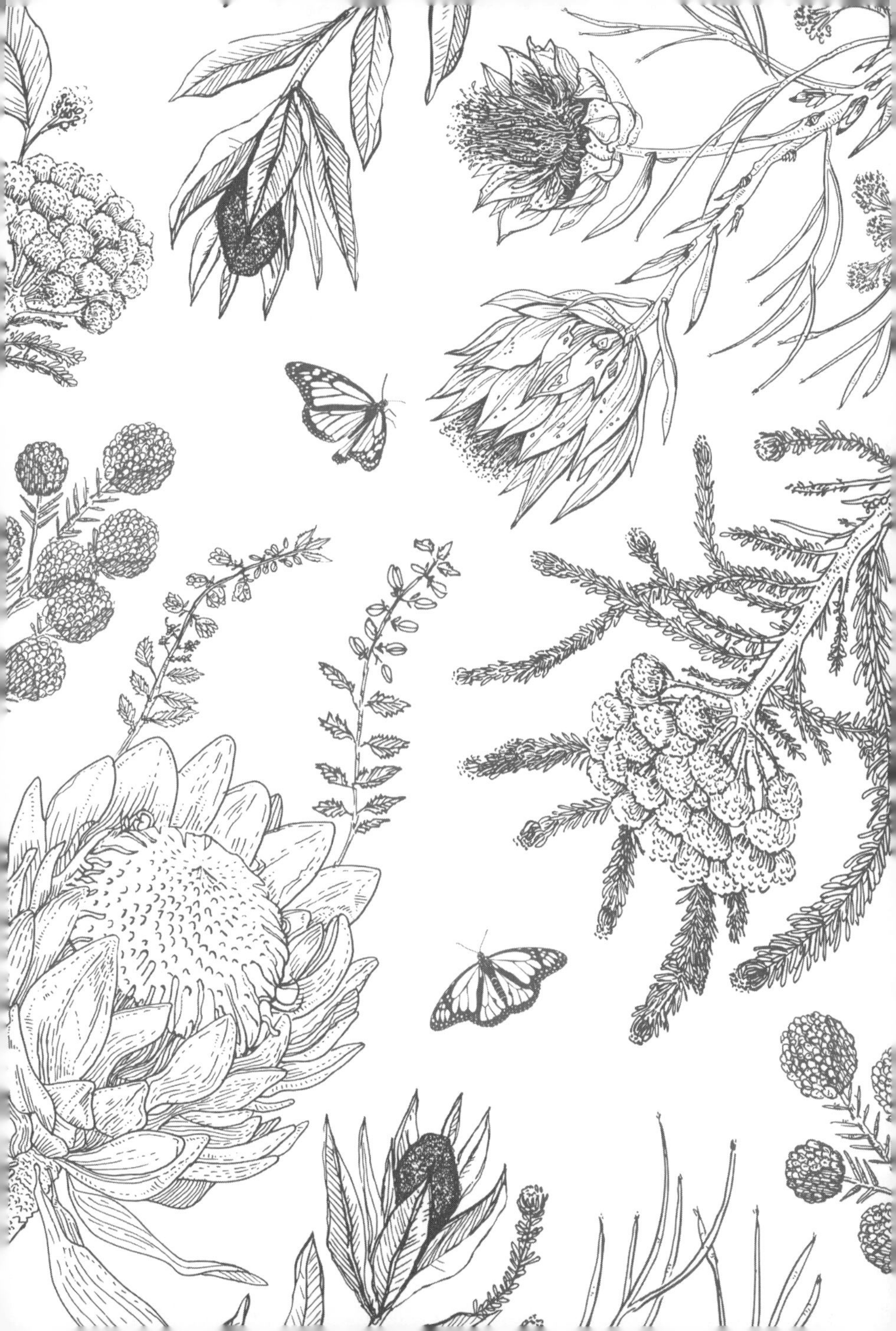

BECAUSE OF
WHO
GOD IS

WEEK NO. 11

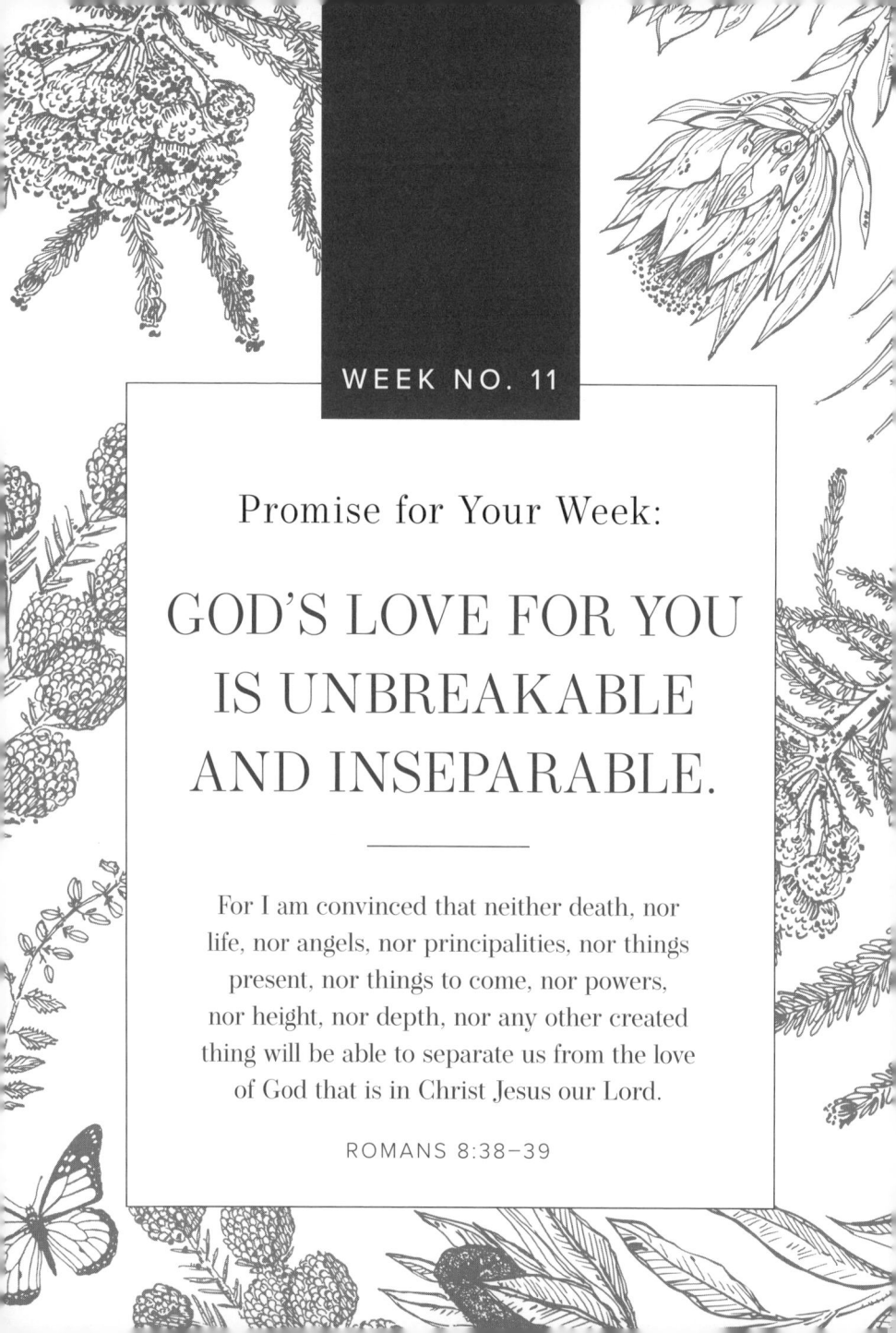

Promise for Your Week:

GOD'S LOVE FOR YOU IS UNBREAKABLE AND INSEPARABLE.

For I am convinced that neither death, nor life, nor angels, nor principalities, nor things present, nor things to come, nor powers, nor height, nor depth, nor any other created thing will be able to separate us from the love of God that is in Christ Jesus our Lord.

ROMANS 8:38–39

DAY 51

PLOT

Relationships are hard. And not just with those we love the most. Every day, we face the challenge of working with, managing, or interacting with other people. Some of these people, perhaps unknowingly, live up to the moniker of "mean girls." They're sweet to your face but cruel behind your back. Passive-aggressive with their not-so-subtle jabs.

Perhaps you know a mean girl—or perhaps you're wondering if you've ever been her.

When I was competing for Miss South Africa, I met incredible women from all over the country, some of whom I am still friends with today. But I certainly had some challenging interactions with a few of them. There were times I tried to join some of the other women during meals or get-togethers, and without saying a word, one or more of them would get up from the table or group and leave. Talk about high school cafeteria vibes! There were other times when I'd fumble over a word during rehearsal or make some sort of flub, and I'd get laughed at for my misstep. They didn't even try to hide, let alone hold back, their mockery.

Some girls even tried to officially boot me out of the competition completely. One time, I was sitting in a van with eleven other contestants on our way to a final fitting with our designers when the air exploded with notifications from our phones. In a matter of seconds, all eyes turned to me, accompanied by giggles and whispers. A group of contestants had tried to get me disqualified on the grounds of having a coach. Although their efforts failed, I felt alone. Judged. Alienated. There I was, in a group of strong, purpose-driven, independent women who were supposed to champion each other, and I felt completely rejected.

In moments like this, it's easy to feel unloved.

Our souls long to belong, to be wholly and unconditionally loved. Think of your childhood best friend. The one who always looked out for you, shared her lunch with you, never betrayed your secrets, and was always there for you. It's comforting to know that a friend who knows you inside and out will have your back. This kind of relationship reminds me a little of our Father in heaven, the One who promised never to leave or forsake us (Hebrews 13:5). The One whose love is greater than we can imagine. The One who guarantees He'll never stop loving us. There is nothing we can do, say, or go through that will change how much He loves us.

Over the next several days, I want you to discover how loved you are.

PRAYER FOR YOUR DAY

God, it's hard when I don't feel like I fit in, when those around me aren't being kind—when even in a room full of people, I feel all alone. I know You didn't create me to live life feeling unloved. You are Love itself. May Your words help me change the way I see myself, the way I see You, and the way I live my life. In Jesus' name I pray, amen.

> **GOD'S LOVE FOR YOU IS UNBREAKABLE AND INSEPARABLE.**

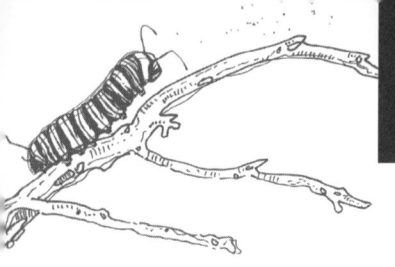

DAY 52

DIG

Today let's spend a few minutes looking inward.

What is that situation, conversation, or encounter with someone that has left you feeling unloved, unwanted, or unwelcome? It may not be a "mean girls" type of experience. Maybe you've never been made fun of, but you're in a marriage where you feel alone. Maybe you grieve the absence of a close connection with your mom or dad because they weren't around or struggled with an addiction or simply were incapable of showing affection.

Write down what happened, how you felt as a result, and some of the lies this experience has led you to believe, such as, "No one will ever love me" or "I'll never be good enough for anyone."

I know this is not easy to do. But digging into the hard places is how we create a space for seeds of healing. After you write down the lies you have believed, I encourage you to write a truth—that you are loved by God.

_____

_____

_____

_____

_____

PRAYER FOR YOU FROM ME

Thank You, Lord, for the woman reading this book. I know You have a purpose and a plan for her life—and they are good ones! I pray she feels Your presence as she writes down the things that may have broken her heart or left her feeling rejected. Comfort her and show her Your love today. In Jesus' name, amen.

> **GOD'S LOVE FOR YOU IS UNBREAKABLE AND INSEPARABLE.**

DAY 53

PLANT

Many of us understand the fundamental truth that God loves us. We sing songs about it. We post about it on social media. We remind friends who are discouraged or overwhelmed that God loves them. We know this truth brings freedom, peace, and security in a fallen world where relationships fail, hearts get broken, and people disappoint us.

But do we spend enough time truly reflecting and meditating on God's love for us as individuals? Think about this for a minute. Have you ever really—*really*—taken God's love for you *personally*? You might be familiar with John 3:16, but now I want you to read it as if God were speaking directly to you.

> "For God so loved ~~the world~~ _____ (insert your name) that He gave His only Son, so that everyone who believes in Him will not perish, but have eternal life."

God doesn't just love the *world*—which is wonderful and amazing—He also loves *you*. It's a wild truth when you really think about it. *You* matter to God. He knows everything about you. He knows when you lost your first tooth, about the failure you had last summer, and your biggest hopes and dreams. Luke 12:7 tells us that God even knows the number of hairs on our heads.

I mentioned earlier how a group of girls were trying to get me ousted from the Miss South Africa competition. Later, after I had become Miss Universe, one of the women in that group invited me to coffee and apologized for participating in that ordeal and for not trusting God's plan for my life, or for her life. It was a beautiful, genuine conversation in which God reminded me that it's only in Him that we find complete and everlasting love. The kind of love that gives us confidence even when those around us are not kind or loving. The kind of love that can never be taken from us.

Romans 8:38–39 reminds us that God loves us with an unbreakable and inseparable love. Your Father in heaven loves you in a way that no one else can. Understanding His love for you changes everything. It may not take away the sting when others make you feel like you don't belong, but it will give you confidence no human love can ever bring.

PRAYER FOR YOUR DAY

God, show me the kind of love You came to this earth to bring and model for us. May I know and share the love that You personally have for me. In Jesus' name, amen.

> **GOD'S LOVE FOR YOU IS UNBREAKABLE AND INSEPARABLE.**

DAY 54

GROW

The author of the book of Romans was a man named Paul. Once a prominent religious figure in the Jewish community, he became a Christ follower after a literal come-to-Jesus moment. Paul studied for about three years and then began spreading the good news to the first-century world. He also encouraged believers to strengthen their faith and cast their vision on eternal, not temporary, things. Paul founded several churches, wrote at least thirteen books in the New Testament, and is known as one of the most influential Christians in history. But there is more to his story than accolades. Paul also went through many hard times.

Because of his unapologetic faith, Paul was under constant persecution. He was beaten, stoned, and jailed multiple times (Acts 14:19; 16:23; 25:14). He survived not one, not two, but three shipwrecks (2 Corinthians 11:25). He was gossiped about, made fun of, and was the victim of death threats. This is the same man who penned the words,

> For I am convinced that neither death, nor life, nor angels, nor principalities, nor things present, nor things to come, nor powers, nor height, nor depth, nor any other created thing will be able to separate us from the love of God that is in Christ Jesus our Lord. (Romans 8:38–39)

If anyone could attest to God's faithful love, it was Paul. Because of his continual hardships, it may have looked on the outside like

God had abandoned him. I mean, who lives through three shipwrecks without having their faith tested? But these terrible circumstances didn't incite Paul to doubt God's love for him; instead, they served to embolden his faith. This is what happens when you personally know and understand God's love for you.

You don't have to do anything more or less for God to love you. He loves you when things are great. He loves you when life is hard. He loves you when you hit all your goals. He loves you when you mess up. He loves you when you're surrounded by people who encourage you. And He loves you when no one is around. God's love is perfect, and it is for *you*!

PRAYER FOR YOUR DAY

Dear God, thank You for loving me the way I am, no matter if I am in good fortune or destitute. No matter how high I climb or how far I fall. Thank You that Your love will never change. In Jesus' name, amen.

> **GOD'S LOVE FOR YOU IS UNBREAKABLE AND INSEPARABLE.**

DAY 55

FLOURISH

Read, meditate on, and memorize Romans 8:38–39. Build your confidence in God's love for you by reflecting on these truths.

- **God's love is faithful.** Psalm 136:2 says, "Give thanks to the God of gods, for His faithfulness is everlasting." God guides, protects, and provides for you.
- **In Christ, you are made new.** Second Corinthians 5:17 says, "Therefore if anyone is in Christ, this person is a new creation; the old things passed away; behold, new things have come." God renews you.
- **God promises His presence.** In Matthew 28:20, Jesus assured, "Follow all that I commanded you; and behold, I am with you always, to the end of the age." You are never alone.
- **Victory is yours through Jesus.** Romans 8:37 declares, "But in all these things we overwhelmingly conquer through Him who loved us." No matter what, through Jesus you will overcome.

What is one thing you can do to remember God's unbreakable and inseparable love for you?

PRAYER FOR YOUR DAY

Father, please be patient with me as I grow in Your ways. In Jesus' name I pray, amen.

GOD'S LOVE FOR YOU IS UNBREAKABLE AND INSEPARABLE.

WEEK NO. 12

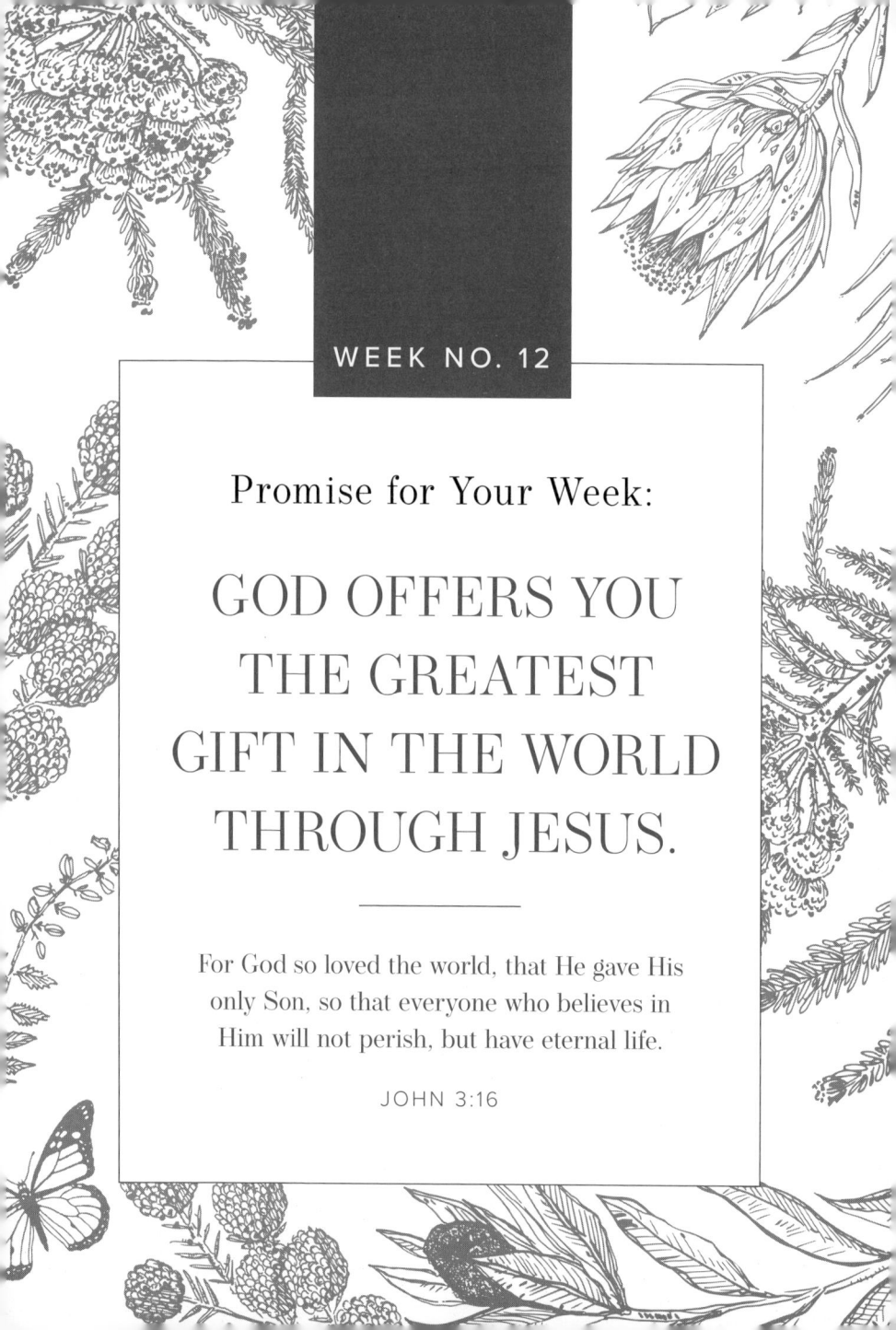

Promise for Your Week:

GOD OFFERS YOU THE GREATEST GIFT IN THE WORLD THROUGH JESUS.

For God so loved the world, that He gave His only Son, so that everyone who believes in Him will not perish, but have eternal life.

JOHN 3:16

DAY 56

PLOT

My faith journey was uniquely shaped by my parents' divorce when I was a baby. I grew up splitting my time between two households—and, consequently, two different churches. Here in the southern United States, a church sits on every other block. But in South Africa, even though about 80 percent of the people profess to belong to the Christian faith, both my parents lived in relatively small towns where church options were somewhat limited. It was hard to get plugged in.

While I deeply valued my parents' faith, there were times when I'd get confused about theology. The teachings varied from one church to the other. One church preached you had to do this and that to go to heaven, and the other church taught a different message. I wasn't sure which was right. Apparently, when I was four, I asked my stepmom to pull to the side of the road so I could ask Jesus into my heart, but I don't have any memory of that moment. I grew up believing in Jesus, but because of my confusion about theology, I always wondered if I would go to heaven one day.

When I attended boarding school at age thirteen, I began to form my own relationship with Jesus without the noise of different church voices. However, it wasn't until I was seventeen that I made an official commitment to Jesus Christ.

It happened at the end of eleventh grade when a fellow classmate suddenly passed away. We learned of the devastating news right before our final math exams. Under the direction of our student pastor, my classmates and I assembled on the sports field to pray. During that moment, the student pastor gave us an opportunity to put our faith in Jesus. I, for one, did not want to question any longer where I was going to spend eternity. I said yes, and it was the best decision I ever made.

I've since learned that going to heaven is only part of the gift of salvation. It's also about connecting with the God who created the universe, becoming more like His Son, Jesus (through the process of sanctification), and loving and serving Him and others. Salvation is an assurance that we are forever deeply loved. My relationship with Jesus shifted from being rooted in the fear caused by confusion to the freedom found in His promises.

Have you ever torn open a gift, expecting one thing, only to find something totally unexpected? This reminds me of our journey with God, especially when it comes to understanding the incredible gift of salvation. When we first come to Christ, many of us have little knowledge of what eternal life with God means. But as our faith grows, it takes on a deeper meaning. This week I'm going to walk alongside you as we uncover what the beautiful gift of salvation is all about.

PRAYER FOR YOUR DAY

Dear Lord, thank You for the promise of eternity, a gift of forever joy in Your presence. Guide me to live with heaven in my heart, knowing each step on earth is part of a journey toward my true, forever home. In Jesus' name, amen.

> **GOD OFFERS YOU THE GREATEST GIFT IN THE WORLD THROUGH JESUS.**

DAY 57

DIG

In the journey of faith, the moment we come to know and accept Jesus as our personal Savior is a pivotal point of transformation and hope. It's a deeply personal experience.

Today I want to give you space to reflect on the moment you committed your life to Jesus. What were the circumstances leading up to this life-changing moment? Describe the feelings, thoughts, and perhaps even the challenges that surrounded this experience. How has your life changed since that day?

_____

_____

_____

_____

_____

If you have not yet chosen Jesus as your Lord and Savior but desire a personal relationship with your Maker, you can do this right now. There is no magic prayer or formula to make this happen. The Bible says, "If you declare with your mouth, 'Jesus is Lord,' and believe in your heart that God raised him from the dead, you will be saved" (Romans 10:9 NIV). All it takes is you asking Him into your life. You can do so by praying what I've written here, or you can use your own words.

Even if you have been walking with Jesus for a while now, I invite you also to read this prayer as a reminder of who our God is and why He loves you so much!

PRAYER FOR YOUR DAY

Jesus, I believe You are God's Son and that You died on the cross to rescue me from sin and eternal death, and to restore my relationship with my Creator. There is nothing I can do or achieve to earn my place in heaven. My place in heaven is a gift and unmerited favor as a result of Your grace. Thank You for forgiving me of all that I've done wrong. I now ask You to take Your rightful place in my life as my Savior and Lord. Live in my heart, fill me with Your love, and help me become the person You have created me to be. Thank You for preparing a place for me in heaven to live with You forever. In Jesus' name, amen.

> **GOD OFFERS YOU THE GREATEST GIFT IN THE WORLD THROUGH JESUS.**

DAY 58

PLANT

Are you ready to plant something deep in your heart? John 3:16 is one of the most well-known passages of Scripture. You've probably heard it many times before, but I want you to read it with fresh ears and fresh soil:

> For God so loved the world, that He gave His only Son, so that everyone who believes in Him will not perish, but have eternal life.

This verse is the foundation for the entire biblical narrative. Packed with spiritual substance, it reveals the rescue mission Jesus has for humankind. This week we're going to do something a little different and take two days to unpack this verse section by section.

- **For God so loved the world:** God's definition of *love* and our world's definition of *love* are as different as day and night. The love we humans know and understand is typically based on feelings, which we all know fluctuate wildly. One day we feel love for our spouse; the next day that same feeling morphs into annoyance. God's love, on the other hand, is an unending ocean, boundless and deep. It knows no conditions, no boundaries, and no end.

  We also throw the word *love* around so much that it loses its meaning. We say we love pizza, the handbag we've been eyeing all year, or our bestie's balayage. But God's love for humankind transcends all of this. It is unearned and undeserved. It is patient and kind (1 Corinthians 13:4). It is eternal. And as the Bible declares, God *is* love (1 John 4:8).

- **That He gave His only Son:** The truth that God gave His most precious gift, His only child, Jesus, underpins the depth of God's commitment to our eternal well-being. Bible scholar Matthew Henry said this about the sacrifice that God willingly made:

> He [God] not only sent him [Jesus] into the world with full and ample power to negotiate a peace between heaven and earth, but he *gave him*, that is, he gave him up to suffer and die for us, as the great propitiation or expiatory sacrifice.[15]

God the Father loved you so much that He made the greatest sacrifice for you. Not only did He send His only Son into the world, but God sent Jesus to die on a cross. God's love for us isn't an empty promise. He put His words into action. Think about what this says about your worth. You are immeasurable in the eyes of God! He deemed you worthy of His greatest sacrifice. God would have sent Jesus to die for you, even if you were the only person in this world!

As we close our time together, hold tight to the truth that you are deeply loved by God.

PRAYER FOR YOUR DAY

God, I thank You for Your sacrificial love, for giving Your Son for us. Help me to live in gratitude, to cherish Your gift, and to reflect Your love in all that I do. In Jesus' name, amen.

GOD OFFERS YOU THE GREATEST GIFT IN THE WORLD THROUGH JESUS.

DAY 59

GROW

Salvation isn't just a gift in God's incredible display of love for us—it also leads to our growth toward a flourishing life. John 3:16 ends with: "So that everyone who believes in Him will not perish, but have eternal life." These fourteen words contain a promise so profound that it transforms lives.

Believing in God is more than acknowledging that He exists; it's about trusting in His love, His grace, and His plans for us. It's understanding that our identity isn't based on ourselves or what the world tells us; who we are comes from God's love and sacrifice for us.

Yes, when we believe, we are promised eternal life with God in heaven. But salvation is more than that. It's about making an eternal impact through what we do in this life on earth. When we accept God's greatest gift of salvation, we are invited into a new way of living, a way that offers forgiveness, redemption, and transformation.

The best part is that this gift isn't based on our perfection, our achievements, our zip code, or our financial status. It's a *free gift*. We don't do anything to earn it. You might feel pressure from society or peers to fit in or be accepted, but this isn't the case with God. He loves you unconditionally. Nothing you do or don't do will ever change His love for you.

Let this verse move you to see life beyond the temporary. Let it be a source of strength, hope, and courage as you navigate challenges, heartbreak, or the unknown. You are loved, forever and always.

PRAYER FOR YOUR DAY

Heavenly Father, help me to be eternally minded, anchored in Your boundless love. Help me to understand my worth in You so my journey in this life is filled with grace, so I reflect Your love in everything I do, and so my life counts for Your kingdom. In Jesus' name, amen.

> **GOD OFFERS YOU THE GREATEST GIFT IN THE WORLD THROUGH JESUS.**

DAY 60

FLOURISH

Today let's read, meditate on, and memorize John 3:16.

To every woman reading this: Remember that believing in God and in His Son, Jesus, changes everything. It means you're never alone, never without purpose, never without love, and you are eternally secure. Your journey may have highs and lows, but His promise remains the same—believe in Him and you will have eternal life. Whatever is causing your heart to doubt or question, rest in this promise. It will change your life.

How does knowing you are deeply loved by God change the way you face challenges and interact with others?

PRAYER FOR YOUR DAY

Jesus, thank You for Your love. Thank You for not just loving me as the world loves things, but being willing to sacrifice everything that You are owed as the Creator of the world for the sake of redeeming me with Your blood. Bring things to my mind today that remind me of how You love me. I do not deserve this type of love from You, which is why I love You all the more. In Christ's name I pray, Amen.

GOD OFFERS YOU THE GREATEST GIFT IN THE WORLD THROUGH JESUS.

WEEK NO. 13

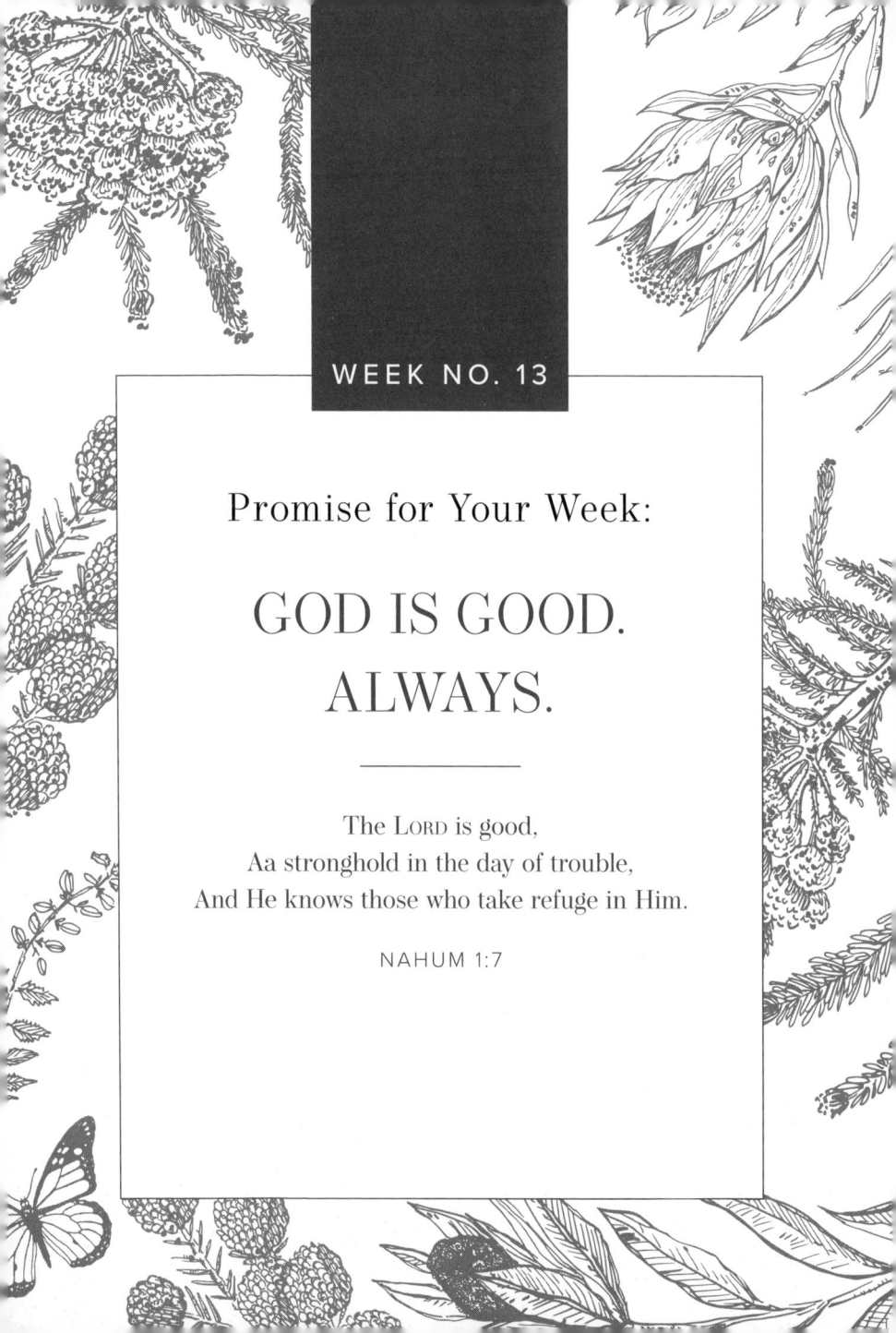

Promise for Your Week:

GOD IS GOOD.
ALWAYS.

The LORD is good,
A stronghold in the day of trouble,
And He knows those who take refuge in Him.

NAHUM 1:7

DAY 61

PLOT

My sister Franje's heartbreaking diagnosis rattled my faith in so many ways. I deeply questioned why God would allow her to be born with such a devastating diagnosis, one with no cure and a short life expectancy. As I became a teenager, I was angry at the thought of her physical suffering, and my heart broke to see my parents so utterly helpless. I also felt like a failure as a big sister since I couldn't do much for Franje. I certainly couldn't make her feel better or cure her illness. And no matter how hard I tried to be a good girl by not creating any additional problems for my parents, or asking for any extravagant things like big birthday parties, I couldn't minimize the responsibilities my father and stepmother had to juggle while providing round-the-clock care for Franje.

Recently, I stumbled across an account of Mother Teresa's life and what she called her "dark night of the soul." That sounds pretty intense, doesn't it? A collection of Mother Teresa's own private writings published in *Come Be My Light* detail her time of feeling distant from God, an experience that lasted for years. Imagine dedicating your life to service and feeling a disconnect between you and the One who has called you to serve. But despite her doubts and questions, her faith endured. A man once approached Mother Teresa with a prayer request for clarity. She refused and said, "I have never had clarity. What I always had is trust. So I will pray that you trust God."[16]

This hit me hard. Like Mother Teresa, I was experiencing my own dark night of the soul, a time of doubt where it felt like I was shouting into the void. It seemed like God was absent, that He was not listening, or maybe that He didn't care at all. But as I learned when navigating Franje's health crisis and discovered later through Mother Teresa's experience, faith isn't always about feeling blessed and connected. Sometimes it's about holding on, even when you feel like letting go. It's about serving, loving, and giving, even when you're not sure what you believe in.

Trusting God isn't always easy. When we get frustrated or discouraged by a certain outcome or a prayer that isn't getting answered the way we want, we may be tempted to question God's character. We may doubt that He is good or trustworthy. But as we embrace these dark nights of the soul while continuing to believe that He has a purpose for us, our faith gets stronger. If we let them, struggles often lead us to our greatest growth and impact. And they can help us see God clearly for who He is. He is good. Always.

PRAYER FOR YOUR DAY

God, remind me that You always have a purpose and a plan in motion, one of hope and a good future. Grant me strength and faith to trust in Your path, no matter how hard it is to walk on. Thank You for never letting me go. In Jesus' name, amen.

GOD IS GOOD. ALWAYS.

DAY 62

DIG

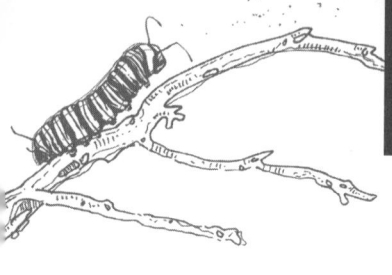

Have you ever poured out your heart to God on paper, crafting a prayer with ink? This might not be your regular practice. Instead, maybe you pray by yourself in the morning or with others at dinnertime. Often we find comfort in our familiar routines, but embracing a new approach, like writing down our prayers, can give us a renewed perspective.

Today write a letter to God expressing your thoughts and feelings. Here are some prompts to help guide you:

- Start your letter by expressing gratitude for God's unchanging presence. Acknowledge how sensing God's presence has impacted you.
- Write down times when you've struggled to see God's goodness.
- Share the lessons you've learned about who God is through different seasons of your life. How have these lessons shaped your relationship with Him?
- Ask for God's guidance in deepening your understanding of His character.
- Reflect on how you've experienced God's love and mercy personally. Consider times when you might not have deserved kindness, yet God showed you unparalleled love and forgiveness.
- Share your hopes and dreams. How does trusting in God's nature shape your expectations for the future?

A PRAYER FOR YOU FROM ME

God, as this reader comes to You with an open heart and mind, give her the courage to face her deepest questions. May she find in You a safe space for exploration—a place where doubts and fears are met with Your grace and understanding. In Jesus' name, amen.

GOD IS GOOD. ALWAYS.

DAY 63

PLANT

If you've been in church long enough, you're probably familiar with the biblical story of Jonah, the prophet God commanded to go to the city of Nineveh to preach repentance. Jonah eventually obeyed, but not before he tried to run away from his calling and, in the process, got swallowed and spit out by a great fish.

Nahum was a prophet after Jonah's time who continued the message of repentance to Nineveh. Nahum showed up at a dark time in the history of the Israelites. Ruled by King Manasseh, they had, once again, turned their back on God. Though Nahum's prophecies foretold impending judgment, he simultaneously delivered hope, giving the people glimpses of God's patience, love, and the promise of revival.

Nahum 1:7 reflects this latter comfort. The prophet wrote, "The LORD is good, a stronghold in the day of trouble, and He knows those who take refuge in Him." I want to focus on the phrase "the LORD is good." God doesn't promise a life free of trouble and trial, but He promises steadfastness of character: He is good. What would it look like if you were to lean into the unchanging nature of God's goodness instead of reverting to unbelief or questioning it?

God's goodness isn't a passive attribute; it's an active, encompassing presence that seeks us out in our darkest hours. It's a goodness that doesn't ignore our pain but enters into it with us, offering strength, comfort, and a way forward. When life doesn't seem good, when our circumstances challenge our peace and cause us to question our faith,

Nahum reminds us that our perception of goodness should be anchored in the unmovable reality of who God is.

And, friend, He is good. All the time.

PRAYER FOR YOUR DAY

Dear Lord, help me embrace Your goodness, even when shadows fall. Open my heart to trust in You, dispel my doubts, and guide me to see Your love and grace in every moment. In Jesus' name, amen.

GOD IS GOOD. ALWAYS.

DAY 64

GROW

It's easy to acknowledge God's goodness when we get the promotion, when we're posting beach selfies while on vacation, or when our household is running smoothly and our fridge doesn't need to be repaired. Yet the true depth of our conviction that God is good is tested not when we're floating in smooth seas, but in the unpredictability and challenges of life.

When our "good" life shifts in the blink of an eye, we must face the question of whether God is truly good or not. He is. Always. Scripture tells us that the Lord does not change (Malachi 3:6), that He is the same yesterday, today, and forever (Hebrews 13:8). Why is this important? Because if the Bible tells us He is good and He doesn't change, He's still good when our hearts get broken. When we fail the exam. When our marriage is crumbling. And He will always be good. We can count on this promise no matter what life throws our way.

The Enemy has sown doubt about God's character ever since he tempted Eve by convincing her to eat from the forbidden tree in the garden of Eden (Genesis 3). He hasn't stopped since, using our vulnerabilities to try and shake our faith. *If God is good, why did He allow that abusive relationship?* he whispers. *Or your child to get sick? Or you to lose your job?* Knowing that deception is the Enemy's game plan should motivate us to remain vigilant. To always hold not just in our hearts but also in our minds the unwavering promise of God's goodness.

Today—and any time you're tempted to question God's good character—declare these truths out loud:

God's goodness surrounds me.
God's goodness is my strength, my shield, my refuge, and my light.
God's goodness is at work in my life.
God's goodness is shaping my future.

Remember, God is good, always.

PRAYER FOR YOUR DAY

Heavenly Father, equip me to counter the Enemy's lies with the solid truth of Your Word. Remind me daily that You are who You say You are—faithful, loving, and unchanging. In Jesus' name, amen.

GOD IS GOOD. ALWAYS.

DAY 65

FLOURISH

Today let's read, meditate on, and memorize Nahum 1:7.

Scripture mapping helps you explore the Bible more intimately by taking a single verse or passage and examining it to uncover deeper meanings, cross-references, word studies, and personal applications. All you need is a Bible (multiple translations), a notebook/journal, colored pens/pencils, and a Bible commentary/study app.[17] Let's get started.

1. Pray for the Holy Spirit to guide your understanding.
2. Write down Nahum 1:7 with its different translations.
3. Break down the verse into smaller keywords. Use a concordance to find the original Hebrew meaning and note any nuances.
4. Cross-reference. Using your Bible or a study app, find and write down other scriptures that echo these themes.
5. Reflect on what Nahum 1:7 means for you personally.
6. Get creative. Express what you've learned through art.

Instead of seeing challenges as unconquerable mountains, view them as landscapes where God can show off His goodness.

A PRAYER FOR YOU FROM ME

Lord, give this reader grace along this lifelong journey of knowing You better each day. Amen.

GOD IS GOOD. ALWAYS.

WEEK NO. 14

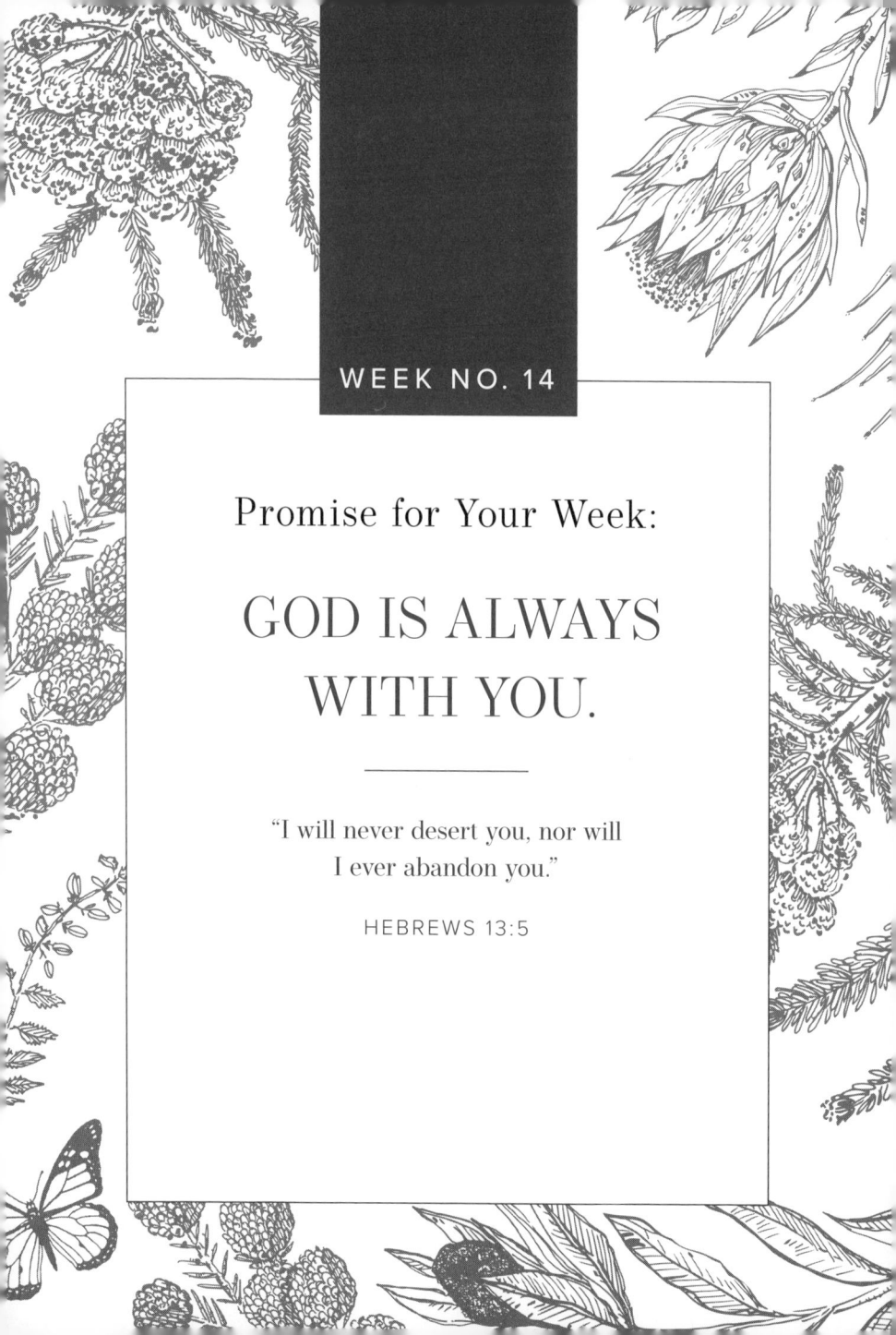

Promise for Your Week:

GOD IS ALWAYS WITH YOU.

"I will never desert you, nor will I ever abandon you."

HEBREWS 13:5

DAY 66

PLOT

South Africa is one of the most beautiful countries in the world. I know I'm probably biased, but the diversity in the landscape, ranging from stretches of dry desert in the Karoo to the luscious forestry of the Garden Route, is unparalleled. We have mountains accompanied by beaches, marine wildlife, wildflowers, and endlessly starry skies as natural decorations.

Unfortunately, though, the crime rate is about 54 percent higher than that of the United States.[18] When I was growing up, our house was surrounded by six-foot walls, security fencing, and an alarm system. Even with all these protections, there was one fear I struggled with: I'm afraid of the dark. This fear was heightened even before I was carjacked (which I'll share more about later this week). I would be fine during the day, but when the sun set, my stomach would knot, my heart would race, and my palms would start to sweat.

Since getting married and moving to the United States where the crime rate is significantly lower, I've gotten better at managing my fear of the dark, but it was quite the adjustment. Coming from a home that necessitated somewhat of a fortress to prevent uninvited people from looking into or entering our home to a house with no fencing or security gates was weird. Never mind a front door with one lock rather than many!

It turns out I'm not alone. One of the most common fears people experience is a fear of the dark. We often think it's just kids who struggle with this, but adults are not immune. While it's true that about three out of four kids are afraid of the dark,[19] before the pandemic, about 11 percent of grown-ups feared darkness. And after COVID, the number increased.[20]

Fear of the dark is a primal instinct that can grip us at any age. Whether it's the fear of the unknown lurking in the shadows or the vulnerability that comes with diminished visibility, the darkness has a way of stirring up our deepest anxieties. Fear is a powerful emotion that can grip our hearts and minds, often leaving us paralyzed and overwhelmed. In the quiet of the night, when shadows dance and whispers echo, fear often finds its breeding ground. The darkness envelops us, and our minds conjure up all manner of phantoms, real or imagined. It's in these moments that our faith is tested, where we must confront our deepest fears and lean on the promises of God.

You may not be afraid of the dark, but you certainly struggle with fears. Perhaps it's the fear of being alone, not having enough money, an unknown future, what others think, failing a class. As followers of Christ, we are called to live not in fear but in faith. This week we will explore how we can find courage in the darkness and overcome our fear with the light of God's presence.

PRAYER FOR YOUR DAY

God, there are things I am afraid of. I'm so grateful You already know what they are. I know that in and with You, there is nothing I need to be afraid of. I pray that You would remind me to trust in You, even when my fears overwhelm me. In Jesus' name I pray, amen.

GOD IS ALWAYS WITH YOU.

DAY 67

DIG

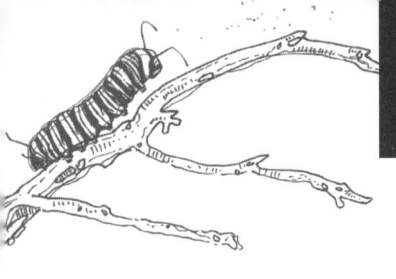

Fear is a universal human experience that can manifest in various ways and affect individuals differently. Today I want you to spend a few minutes thinking about what scares you the most. Answer the following questions as best as you can:

What are some situations or experiences that trigger fear for you?

___

How do you typically respond when you feel afraid?

___

Are there any recurring patterns or themes in your fears?

___

Have you ever tried to confront your fears? If so, what was that experience like?

_____

_____

Can you trace the origin of your fear to a specific event or circumstance in your past?

_____

_____

I know it can be daunting to step out of your comfort zone and confront the things that scare you. But I also know that, as Christians, we have a faith that can move mountains and a God who promises never to leave us nor forsake us. There is power in verbally calling out the lies the Enemy uses for evil and crushing them with the truth and power of God's promises.

A PRAYER FOR YOU FROM ME

Heavenly Father, I pray for the woman reading this book. I believe in her ability through You to navigate and overcome her fears and emerge victorious on the other side. And, most importantly, I believe in the power of Your love to carry her through even the darkest of times. I pray she feels Your presence in her life. In Jesus' name, amen.

GOD IS ALWAYS WITH YOU.

DAY 68

PLANT

My fear of darkness was exacerbated after I got carjacked in Johannesburg, South Africa, in 2017. As the current Miss South Africa, I sat in my car at a red traffic light, all dressed up on my way to an event. Suddenly, multiple men, some of whom were armed, surrounded me. I tried to get away, but one man grabbed me and tried to push me back into the car, yelling something like, "Get in, you're going with us!" In a split-second decision, I punched the guy as hard as I could in his throat. It gave me just enough time to run. As I fled down a traffic-filled avenue, begging for someone to help me, no one would. Finally, a young woman unlocked her car door and offered me an escape. I'll be forever grateful to her.*

I vividly remember the first time I took a shower after this traumatic experience. I was so scared to shampoo my hair because it meant I had to close my eyes. Not only that, but I was terrified to fall asleep at night! It's been a long, hard road as I've navigated this fear, but prayer and therapy have done wonders for me over the years. I also know that God didn't create me to be afraid.

The one thing that has helped quell my fear is the promise God gives in Hebrews 13:5: "I will never desert you, nor will I ever abandon you."

This powerful promise reminds me that I am never alone, even in the darkest of times. God is with us, guiding us, strengthening us, and

---

* Note: You can find the full story of this carjacking in my book *A Crown That Lasts*.

upholding us with His righteous hand. In a world filled with uncertainty and turmoil, fear often finds its way into our hearts and minds. Yet, as followers of Christ, we are called to a different posture—a posture of faith, trust, and unwavering confidence in the God who promises to be with us always.

No matter how tightly fear grips your heart, you can be confident that you are never alone. God is with you every step of the way. He wants to replace your fears with the kind of peace and joy that only He can offer. He longs for you to trust that He is faithful, that His promises are true, that He will never leave you. I encourage you today to turn to Him when fear grips your heart. Lean into the promise of His presence.

PRAYER FOR YOUR DAY

Thank You, Father, for the gift of Your presence. May we never take it for granted. Instead, teach us to cling to it with all our hearts, knowing that You are the source of our strength and hope. In Jesus' name, amen.

GOD IS ALWAYS WITH YOU.

DAY 69

GROW

God's presence is like a beacon of light in the darkness, dispelling our fears and illuminating the path ahead. When we fix our eyes on Him, our fears fade away in the brilliance of His light. In Psalm 27:1, David wrote, "The Lord is my light and my salvation; whom should I fear?" David was the young shepherd boy who killed Goliath and was chosen by God to lead the nation of Israel. But David didn't become king until years later, well after he was hunted down by King Saul, who was already in charge. David endured death threats from the most powerful man in Israel yet kept His trust in God. Can we have that same courage? Yes!

So how do we practically apply the promise that God is always with us when we find ourselves in the dark? Here are three ways:

1. **Pray.** When we feel afraid, we can turn to God, pouring out our hearts to Him and seeking His comfort and peace. We can talk to Him anytime, anywhere. Instead of allowing fear to saturate our spirit, we can come to Him and tell Him our fears.
2. **Read the Bible.** The Word of God is a powerful weapon against fear, as it reminds us of God's promises and His faithfulness. When we fill our minds with the truth of God's Word, fear loses its grip on our hearts and courage takes its place.

3. **Connect with community.** We are reminded that we are not alone when we surround ourselves with fellow believers who can encourage and support us in our times of fear. The right community can make a world of difference!

As we journey through life, we will undoubtedly experience moments of fear and darkness. But we can take comfort in the knowledge that God is with us. Pray. Read the Bible. Surround yourself with community. The more you do these things, the more you will experience His peace and the less power fear will have over you.

PRAYER FOR YOUR DAY

Father, thank You for Your constant presence in my life. You are my refuge and strength. You are my ever-present help in times of trouble. You are faithful and have promised never to leave me. Thank You for the confidence I can have knowing You will never leave my side. In Jesus' name, amen.

GOD IS ALWAYS WITH YOU.

DAY 70

FLOURISH

Today let's read, meditate on, and memorize Hebrews 13:5. Build confidence in God's presence through reflective journaling. By exploring moments of spiritual growth and answered prayers, you can deepen your awareness of God's presence and faithfulness. Use your reflections to remind you that God has been with you in every season—and He's not going anywhere.

- Think back to a time when you felt particularly aware of God's presence. Journal and describe what stirred that awareness, how it shaped your faith, and its impact on you.
- Recall times when God answered your prayers or provided for you in an unexpected way. Capture the details of those moments and what they revealed about His faithfulness.
- Revisit specific prayers that were answered, big or small, and describe how you recognized God's hand at work.

Remember, the God who goes before you is the same God who walks beside you. No matter what lies ahead, you can face it with confidence.

PRAYER FOR YOUR DAY

Lord, help me to see the world as You do. In Jesus' name, amen.

GOD IS ALWAYS WITH YOU.

WEEK NO. 15

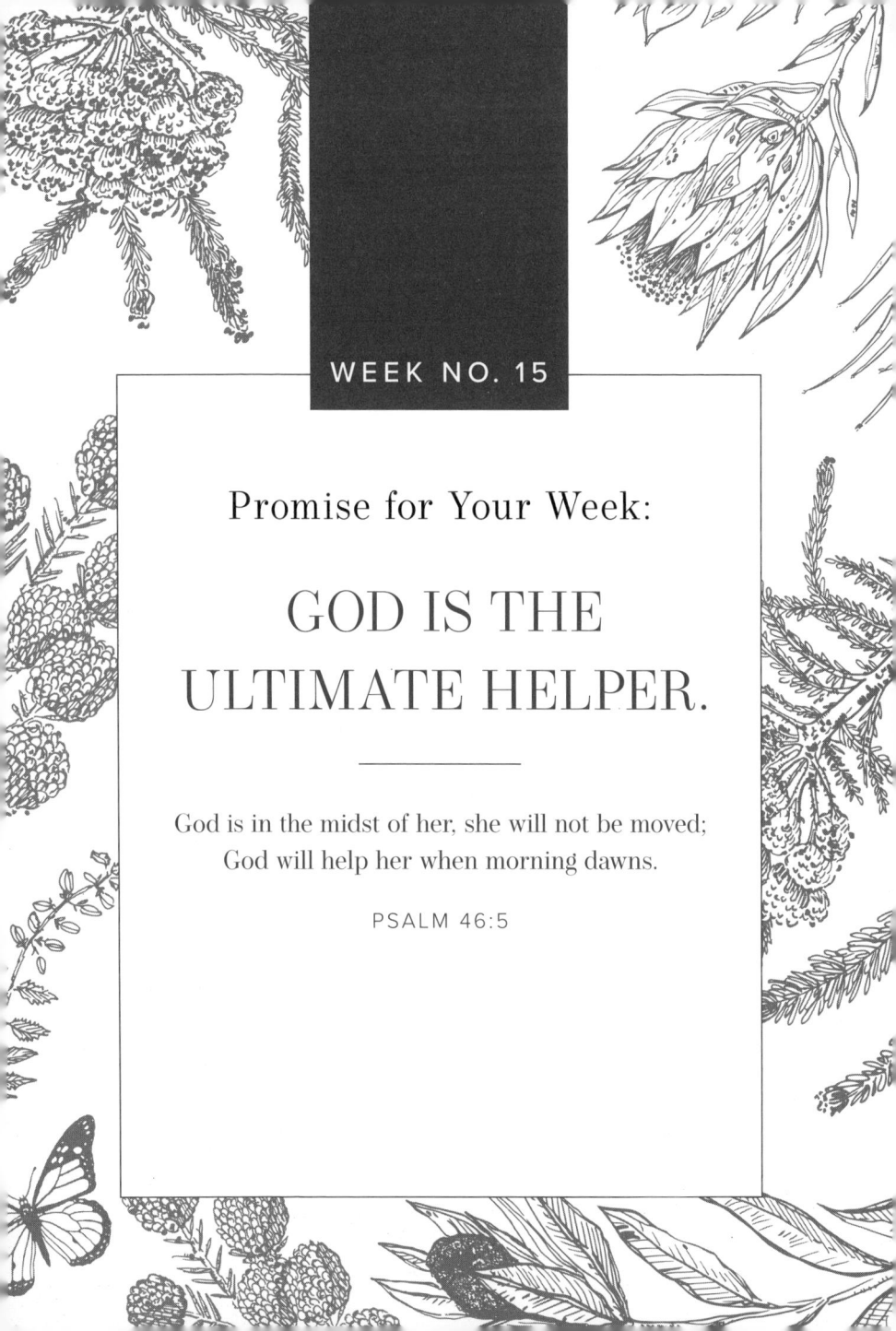

Promise for Your Week:

GOD IS THE ULTIMATE HELPER.

God is in the midst of her, she will not be moved;
God will help her when morning dawns.

PSALM 46:5

DAY 71

PLOT

Earlier I shared about my carjacking experience. Today I want to highlight what happened as I started running away from my attackers, which was even more traumatic than being carjacked.

As I mentioned, my car was stopped on a busy boulevard in bumper-to-bumper traffic. As I took off, I waved down driver after driver, begging for someone to help me. It was broad daylight, and I was dressed in a cocktail dress because I was on my way to an appearance as Miss South Africa. There were families in some of the cars, single drivers, male and female, and couples in others. Each person sitting in the driver's seat saw me pleading for help but did nothing. Some even yelled at me to get away from their car, as if I were a perpetrator. On the one hand, being in a country where carjackings are common, I understood why they were afraid to assist me—people were hesitant to put themselves in harm's way. But in that moment, I didn't understand why no one stopped to help. The drivers all ignored me. Some even turned and looked the other way as I begged them to open the door and let me in. Others rolled up their windows or locked their cars before continuing to ignore my plight.

Eventually, a kind nineteen-year-old girl stopped and invited me into her car. She sped off and drove me to a safe place. I am so grateful for her help. In one of the most chaotic times in my life, a stranger reached out and brought me to safety. Of course you don't have to be carjacked to appreciate the gift of help.

Feeling unsupported, unseen, or even underappreciated can be deeply discouraging. It's in these moments of vulnerability that the longing for support and encouragement becomes most acute. Finding yourself without that help can leave you feeling isolated and disheartened.

At one point or another, we've all been there. Struggling to pass a class, dealing with financial strain, navigating mental health challenges, or experiencing chronic pain are all circumstances in which the absence of help can weigh heavily on us. However, amid the discouragement, it's important to remember that help can come from unexpected places. And reaching out for support, even in vulnerability, can lead to unforeseen blessings and renewed hope.

PRAYER FOR YOUR DAY

Lord, thank You that You always hear our prayers, and thank You for Your faithfulness to answer them according to Your will. Help me to trust in Your perfect timing and to lean on Your unfailing love when I need it most. In Jesus' name, amen.

GOD IS THE ULTIMATE HELPER.

DAY 72

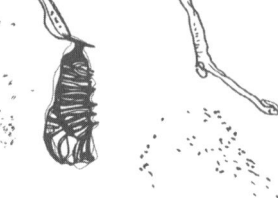

DIG

Do you need help today? For most of us, the answer is yes. Perhaps you want to be a more engaged parent. Or you need help figuring out the direction of your life or paying your tuition bill this semester. Or maybe you have a more internal struggle. Perhaps you need help connecting with Jesus or surrendering a situation or relationship to Him. Please know that help from heaven is here. God will do what it takes to care for you (Matthew 6:26). We'll further explore that truth tomorrow, but for now, sit in the quiet and answer the following questions in preparation:

Have you ever experienced a situation where you felt like your needs or feelings were overlooked? How did it make you feel?

_____

_____

_____

How do you typically cope with feelings of being unseen or unsupported?

_____

_____

_____

What advice would you give to a friend who is experiencing similar feelings of being unnoticed or unsupported?

_____

_____

_____

A PRAYER FOR YOU FROM ME

Dear heavenly Father, I lift up this reader to You in prayer. In the midst of her swirling emotions and tangled thoughts, lead her toward clarity and peace. You know the depths of her heart, the joys and the struggles, the fears and the hopes. Help her, Lord, to sort through these feelings with wisdom and grace. In Jesus' name, amen.

GOD IS THE ULTIMATE HELPER.

DAY 73

PLANT

If you feel the weight of the world on your shoulders today, focus on the comforting truth found in Psalm 46:5:

> God is in the midst of her, she will not be moved;
> God will help her when morning dawns.

As we examine this verse, let's consider a little background: the sons of Korah, descendants of the Levite tribe in ancient Israel, wrote this psalm. When they used the female pronouns *her* and *she*, they weren't actually writing about a woman; they were writing about the nation of Israel. Most scholars believe this scripture was written during a time of national crisis. Though Israel had many enemies who threatened her safety, Psalm 46 heralds the extraordinary power of God to stand for and defend His people. And that is the same powerful God who stands with you today.

God helps us. I know that promises can sometimes come across as trite or cliché, particularly when we are in one of the hardest seasons of our lives. But a promise from God is more than a catchy saying or post-able phrase. It is a tangible reality that we can cling to each day. His promise is the steady anchor amid life's turbulent seas.

How can we experience this promise of God's help?

1. **Lean into your crew.** We are not meant to journey alone. Surround yourself with fellow believers who can encourage,

uplift, and pray for you. Seek out mentors and friends who offer guidance and support in your walk with God. Read a book with a friend. Join a Bible study. Start a support group.
2. **Say "thank you."** Gratitude shifts our focus from what we lack to what we have, filling us with joy and contentment. Cultivate a heart of gratitude by counting your blessings each day. Take time to thank God for what He has done in your life. Think about the ways He has protected and looked after you.
3. **Seek God's presence everywhere you go.** We can seek God anywhere. As you rush to your next class, get ready for the day, or rest your head on your pillow, tune in to God's presence. Rest there for a bit. You don't have to say anything. Recognize in this quiet moment the promise that He is always with you (Psalm 139:7–10).

As you face the challenges and opportunities that lie ahead, remember this truth: You are never alone. God is with you, empowering you, guiding you, and sustaining you every step of the way.

PRAYER FOR YOUR DAY

God, I need You. Today, tomorrow, always. Thank You for the power of Your Word. It is more than a collection of words on a page. It is Your promise to help us. Thank You for being my help. Help me to acknowledge You more and more, especially in circumstances where I may not see or feel Your presence. In Jesus' name, amen.

GOD IS THE ULTIMATE HELPER.

DAY 74

GROW

Has anyone ever inspired you to be a better person? The young woman who drove me to safety after I was carjacked inspired me to be a woman who would always do my best to help someone in need.

There is a synergy between the promise that God helps us and our desire to help others. It's a divine dance that strengthens our faith journey. God doesn't just stop at helping us; He calls us to be His hands and feet in this world, spreading love, kindness, and compassion to those around us. It's like God is saying, "Hey, I've got you covered. Now go out there and be a blessing to others."

When we lend a helping hand to others, we reflect God's heart and extend His love to those in need. Think about how many times God's help has come to you in the form of a friend reaching out at the right time, or a colleague who was able to pitch in for you when you had a personal emergency, or someone who offered you a job during hard times.

Whether it's giving a generous tip to your server, volunteering at a community event, buying extra groceries to give to someone in need, or noticing and talking to that person who most people in society ignore, make the decision today to extend God's help to others.

The divine nudge I experienced after being helped by that young woman snowballed into my participation in the fight against human trafficking. I educated myself on the evil of human trafficking, its prevalence, its exploitation of children, and those who are responsible for this horrific reality. This awareness was a huge wake-up call for me.

Today I get to serve on multiple boards in the United States and overseas for organizations that fight against human trafficking. Being one of many in this battle has been eye-opening and humbling. I often feel insufficient. But God hasn't called any one person to save the world. He has called us to do what we can, where we can, with what we have.

So, as you go about your day, keep your eyes and heart open to opportunities to help others. Look for ways, big or small, to be a light in someone else's darkness.

PRAYER FOR YOUR DAY

Heavenly Father, thank You for Your endless love and support. Give us the courage and compassion to lend a helping hand wherever it's needed. May our actions reflect Your love and bring glory to Your name. In Jesus' name, amen.

GOD IS THE ULTIMATE HELPER.

DAY 75

FLOURISH

Today let's read, meditate on, and memorize Psalm 46:5.

Spend time today reflecting on this verse. If doubt creeps in, try this: Instead of ruminating on what keeps you from believing God helps you, I invite you to focus on a promise found in Scripture. Strengthening your faith is not just about ignoring thoughts or feelings; it's about replacing them with what God says is true.

When your feelings get the best of you, return to Scripture for a reminder of what God says about your situation. God's Word is the ultimate guide to a thriving life.

When I start thinking	I'll remember that
Surrendering to God's plan is scary.	Even when I don't understand His ways, I can trust that He is working all things together for my good (Romans 8:28).
I'm alone in this.	God is always with me; He will never leave or forsake me (Deuteronomy 31:6).
I'll never overcome this struggle.	I can do all things through Christ who strengthens me (Philippians 4:13).

PRAYER FOR YOUR DAY

Lord, instruct me how to live in Your love apart from the lies of this world. In Jesus' name, amen.

GOD IS THE ULTIMATE HELPER.

WEEK NO. 16

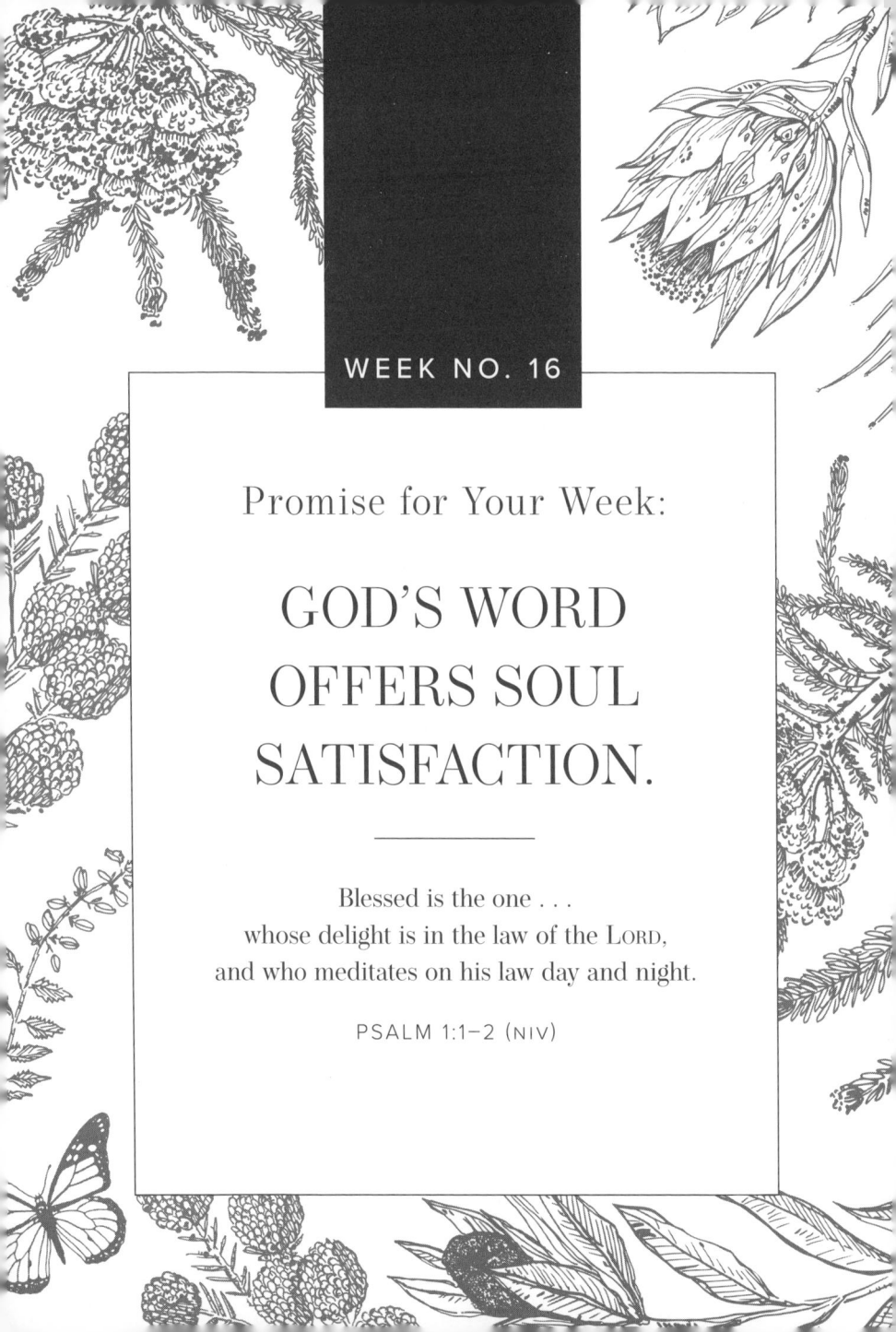

Promise for Your Week:

GOD'S WORD OFFERS SOUL SATISFACTION.

Blessed is the one . . .
whose delight is in the law of the Lord,
and who meditates on his law day and night.

PSALM 1:1–2 (NIV)

DAY 76

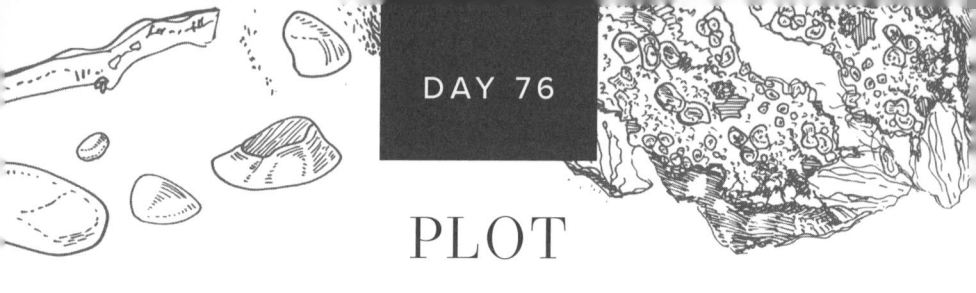

PLOT

Around the time the New Testament was written, there was a special Jewish ceremony on the first day of school where children were given slates with the Hebrew alphabet, two Bible verses,[21] and the phrase "The Torah will be my calling."* The teacher read these words to the child, and then the child repeated them back. Pretty straightforward, right? Except, afterward, the slate was coated with . . . *honey*!

Yes! Delicious, sweet honey! Unable to resist, the child would lick it off, recalling Ezekiel's experience of God's Word tasting as sweet as "honey" (Ezekiel 3:3). Following the ceremony, the child would enjoy sweet cakes with Bible verses from the Torah written on them.[22] For the ancient rabbis, education wasn't just about learning facts but about savoring the sweetness of encountering God's Word. As a girl who loves a sweet treat, I love that illustration!

In Psalm 1:1-2, we see a similar sentiment echoed:

> Blessed is the one
> > who does not walk in step with the wicked
> or stand in the way that sinners take
> > or sit in the company of mockers,
> *but whose delight* is in the law of the LORD,
> > and who meditates on his law day and night. (NIV,
> > > emphasis mine)

---

* Note: The Torah is a traditional way to refer to the first five books of the Old Testament: Genesis, Exodus, Leviticus, Numbers, and Deuteronomy.

Just as the Jewish tradition highlighted the sweetness of God's Word through honey, Psalm 1 emphasizes the satisfaction and delight found in meditating on God's instruction. The Word of God is not merely *informative* but deeply *satisfying* to the soul, providing nourishment and joy as we engage with it.

Now, don't get me wrong—life is full of satisfying things. Like when my thoughtful husband brings me a cup of coffee, when we come home to our excited fur babies after a long trip, or when I see the sunrise on the way to the airport. There's plenty to delight in and thank God for, but this passage should shape how we interact with the Scriptures. Just as the child in the ceremony experienced the sweetness of honey, over the next few days I want us to experience fulfillment and delight in immersing ourselves in the truths of the Bible.

PRAYER FOR YOUR DAY

Lord, thank You for Your Word! To have access to it is truly a gift. May Your Word water my soul and cause growth in my life. May it not just fill my head but also transform my heart. Help me to prioritize Your truth, savor its sweetness, and let it guide my decisions. In Jesus' name, amen.

GOD'S WORD OFFERS SOUL SATISFACTION.

DAY 77

DIG

When you think of the Bible, what are your first thoughts? Even though it was written many years ago, it is not just some dusty old book. It is a timeless, historical, and reliable source of *divine* wisdom and truth. Even more so, it's a love letter from God Himself to you and me!

Written over a period of 1,500 years by more than forty inspired authors from all walks of life, the Bible is beautiful in its one unifying message: God created us for a loving relationship with Him. And for thousands of years, brave men and women have carried this "love letter" through wars, persecutions, natural disasters, plagues, schisms, and everything in between. From generation to generation, the Bible has remained a steadfast anchor, able to satisfy the deepest longings and questions of the human heart. To some it might seem a bit intimidating or dull, but the more you dive into its pages, the more it shapes you into who God created you to be.

Psalm 1:1 begins with "Blessed is the one." This idea of "blessing" is connected to those who "delight" in and "meditate" on God's Word. My father-in-law likes to picture this meditation as a cow chewing its cud. It's a slow, deliberate process. The cow munches on some grass, then swallows it. Later it regurgitates that partially digested food, bringing it back up to chew on it some more (I know . . . gross!). But this repetitive chewing is how a cow gets all the nutrients it needs from the grass.

In this same way, when we *meditate* on the Bible day and night, we're not just quickly reading through it and moving on. Instead, we're like that cow, chewing on scripture slowly and thoughtfully. We read a passage, mull it over in our minds, and let its truths sink deep into our hearts. Then, just like the cow regurgitates its food to chew on again, we bring those truths back to mind throughout our day.

So, let's practice this! Using Psalm 23 as our passage, pick out a translation you like, read it, then read it again, and once you're finished, meditate on these questions:

How does David portray God in this passage? What do you resonate with the most?

_____

_____

How does Psalm 23 shape your attitude toward the Scriptures? Write one truth you'd like to remember throughout your day.

_____

_____

A PRAYER FOR YOU FROM ME

Father, You are the Good Shepherd. Help us to approach Your Word with reverence and humility, knowing that it holds the power to transform our lives and shape us into who You created us to be. May we find hope, comfort, and direction in it, and may Your Word come to mind quickly throughout our day. In Jesus' name, amen.

GOD'S WORD OFFERS SOUL SATISFACTION.

DAY 78

PLANT

In Ephesians 6:17, Paul identified the sword of the Spirit as the Word of God. Later, in Hebrews, we're told, "The word of God is living and active, and sharper than any two-edged sword... able to judge the thoughts and intentions of the heart" (Hebrews 4:12). This imagery of the Word as a sword isn't just metaphorical; it's a powerful reality. Think about Jesus in the wilderness facing temptation. Each time the devil came at Him with lies and deceit, Jesus fought back with Scripture.[23] It was His sword, His weapon of choice. In the same way, the Word is our weapon, our source of strength, and our guide that cuts through doubts, fears, and uncertainties.

I want to introduce you to my version of the SWORD drill.[24] It's a fitting name for a simple tool that helps us get more out of reading the Bible. Let's walk through it together.

> **(S)cripture:** Begin by selecting a passage from the Bible. For today, let's stick with Psalm 23. As you read it again, write down what verse(s) stood out to you.

_____

_____

> **(W)ait:** Take a moment to pause and reflect on the verse you wrote down. Ask the Holy Spirit to guide your thoughts and reveal any insights or convictions.

_____

_____

(O)bserve: Write down anything you notice about this passage. Are there any themes, key ideas, patterns, etc.? What is God saying to you through these verses?

_____

_____

(R)equest: Ask God how you can apply your observations to your life.

_____

_____

(D)eclare: Finally, declare God's promises and truths over your life. Speak them out loud, and share what you've learned with one other person.

By engaging in the SWORD drill regularly, we go from simply *reading* the Bible to *studying* the Bible. Let's commit to making time for Scripture study and meditation, knowing that it is our offensive weapon and our pathway to true satisfaction!

PRAYER FOR YOUR DAY

Father, may Your Word be my go-to, my first choice for comfort, peace, and fulfillment. May it build me up, chisel away what needs to go, and form me into the likeness of Christ. Reveal to me spiritual truth. In Jesus' name, amen.

GOD'S WORD OFFERS SOUL SATISFACTION.

DAY 79

GROW

Let's look again at the first line of Psalm 1: "Blessed is the one."
We sometimes hear people say they're "blessed" to have things—a fulfilling job, a loving family, good health. We may even hear a phrase like "Bless your heart" that is said flippantly and isn't quite a wish for blessing. But have you ever stopped to think about the word *blessed*? In the Bible, it carries a very specific meaning. Old Testament scholar Bruce Waltke argues that when the Bible uses the word *blessed*, it's not so much about feeling good or happy in the present moment. Instead, it's more about looking ahead and realizing the special favor, benefits, or rewards that come from being close to God. Waltke suggests that a better way to understand the beginning of Psalm 1:1 might be "How rewarding" or "How favored."[25]

> [How rewarding/favored] is the one . . . whose delight is in the law of the LORD, and who meditates on his law day and night. (Psalm 1:1–2 NIV)

Now, that makes a little more sense! Very clearly, we see the psalmist linking favor and reward to our joy and effort in God's Word. Simply put, the more we're in the Word, the more we benefit from it.

It's important to note that the favor and reward implied aren't necessarily about gaining material things or living a stress-free life. Instead, they're about our growth as believers. When we delight in God's Word and meditate on it, we're strengthened spiritually, emotionally, and mentally. Our connection to God's truth enables us to navigate life's challenges with resilience and wisdom.

The psalmist painted this picture in even more detail in the next verse by comparing those who delight and meditate in God's instruction to "a tree planted by streams of water, which yields its fruit in season and whose leaf does not wither—whatever they do prospers" (v. 3 NIV).

Just as a tree needs water to grow and thrive, we need the nourishment of God's Word to flourish spiritually. So today, let's commit to being like that tree—rooted deeply in God's Word, drawing sustenance and life from its truth. Let's embrace the rewarding journey of delighting in His law, knowing that as we do, we will grow in every aspect of our lives.

PRAYER FOR YOUR DAY

Dear God, help me grasp the depth of the blessing of Your Word, understanding that it's not just about fleeting happiness but about experiencing Your favor as I walk closely with You. Your Word not only shapes me, but it paints a picture of You. Give me the heart to see Your love on every page. In Jesus' name, amen.

GOD'S WORD OFFERS SOUL SATISFACTION.

DAY 80

FLOURISH

Today let's read, meditate on, and memorize Psalm 1:1–2.

To end this week, I encourage you to sink your roots deep into God's Word. Jesus Himself assured us in the Sermon on the Mount, "I tell you the truth, until heaven and earth disappear, not even the smallest detail of God's law will disappear until its purpose is achieved" (Matthew 5:18 NLT). Jesus is saying that God's Word is here to stay; it's timeless and unchanging. That means you can build your life upon it with complete confidence.

In my hometown of Sedgefield, I was surrounded by towering mountains and lush forests. Whenever I faced challenges, my mom would remind me, "The tallest trees catch the most wind." In other words, the stronger and taller something stands, the more resistance it faces. When we stand tall on God's Word and live out our God-given purpose, we will catch "wind" from the Enemy. But when we're grounded in truth, we can stand firm knowing that God's Word is our weapon.

PRAYER FOR YOUR DAY

Father, teach me Your ways, correct my misunderstandings about Your nature. Teach me who You are and how You operate. Take me deeper into Your Scriptures as I meditate on them. Give me new insights that transform not only my thoughts but my walk with others and You. In Jesus' name, amen.

GOD'S WORD OFFERS SOUL SATISFACTION.

WEEK NO. 17

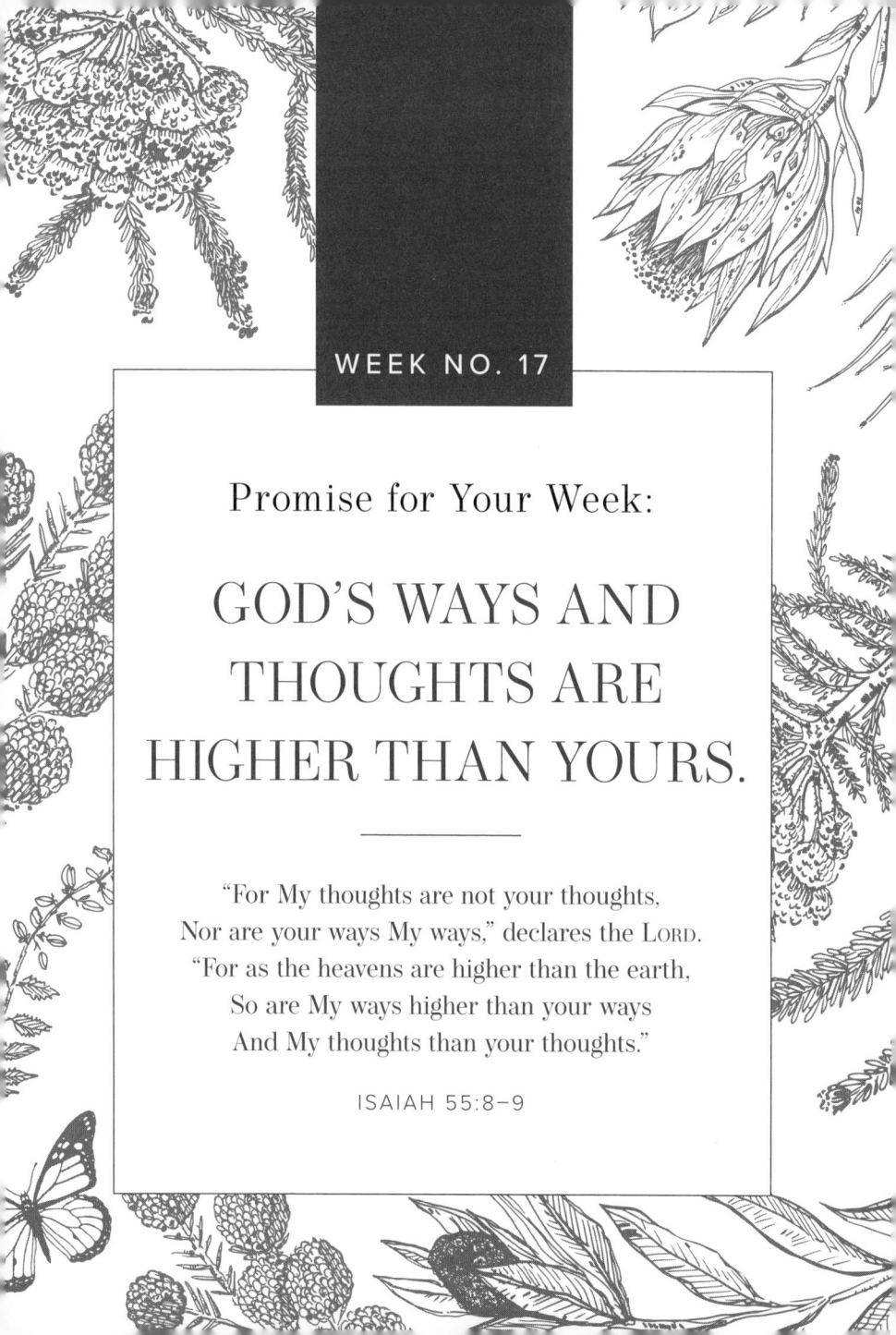

Promise for Your Week:

GOD'S WAYS AND THOUGHTS ARE HIGHER THAN YOURS.

"For My thoughts are not your thoughts,
Nor are your ways My ways," declares the Lord.
"For as the heavens are higher than the earth,
So are My ways higher than your ways
And My thoughts than your thoughts."

ISAIAH 55:8–9

DAY 81

PLOT

The first day after I completed my role as Miss Universe—and many thereafter—was full of unknowns and uncertainties. Everything I owned was stored across four different cities on two different continents. I couldn't remember what was where, so it was difficult to find anything. Since I didn't have a New York state identification, getting a lease for a place to live in New York City was nearly impossible, never mind trying to open my own cell phone account. And although I'd had a blast traveling the world the previous year, I was still recuperating from jet lag. (Don't worry, this is not a whine fest.)

My MO for most of my life had been to plan and execute: Figure out a goal, determine a strategy, and achieve said goal. For the first time in my life, however, I had no dream, no strategy, and no way to achieve a goal I couldn't even envision. Promising projects like modeling were on the horizon, but most would require some form of compromise I wasn't willing to make. Coupled with a string of nos on the projects I *was* interested in, I struggled with feeling stuck. I was lost.

Looking back, I knew I had many lessons to learn. And I'm grateful for the wisdom I've gained. But during this waiting period, the one truth I wish I had held on to was that even if I had no plan or a road map for my future, God was still in control.

Is there an area in your life in which you struggle with not knowing the next step to take? This uncertainty can breed anxiety, unrest, and even shame. Some of us might think there's something wrong with us because we haven't figured out the plan. Maybe we're afraid

God is not answering our prayers the way we want because we did something wrong.

Feeling a bit lost in the maze of life is totally natural. We've all been there, pondering what our grand life plan is supposed to look like. But here's the beautiful part: Even when we're not sure of our next move, God has got it all under control. He's like the ultimate GPS, always guiding us toward our purpose, even when the road seems a bit foggy.

PRAYER FOR YOUR DAY

God, guide my steps and illuminate my path as I journey through life, trusting in Your divine plan for my future. It's tough when I don't know exactly what to do or where to go. Trade my anxieties for peace. I know that You go before me, paving the way with Your perfect love and grace. In Jesus' name, amen.

> **GOD'S WAYS AND THOUGHTS ARE HIGHER THAN YOURS.**

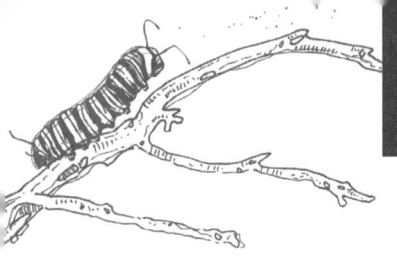

DAY 82

DIG

Uncertainty has a sneaky way of creeping into our lives, especially when it comes to thinking about the future. If you've been feeling a bit overwhelmed lately, I want to remind you that you are not alone in this journey. We all face moments when the path ahead seems hazy and we're not quite sure whether we should move left, right, or stand still. Today I want you to take a few deep breaths and journal based on the following prompts:

Write about an experience where you felt uncertain about your future.

_____

_____

_____

_____

What coping strategies have you used to deal with uncertainty?

_____

_____

_____

_____

How can you proactively navigate uncertainty going forward?

A PRAYER FOR YOU FROM ME

Dear heavenly Father, I lift this reader to You in prayer. May Your comforting presence surround her, easing the burdens of her heart. Remind her that You have a perfect plan and purpose for her life. Guide her steps with Your divine wisdom and grace. Grant her strength and faith to trust in Your unfailing love. In Jesus' name, amen.

> **GOD'S WAYS AND THOUGHTS ARE HIGHER THAN YOURS.**

DAY 83

PLANT

I've learned that no matter how well we calculate, prepare, anticipate, or dream, schedules will get interrupted, timelines delayed, and sometimes our perfectly planned strategies will blow up in our faces. And while the reasons may not make sense to us, one thing is certain: God is still in charge, and He knows what He is doing.

Isaiah 55:8–9 tells us:

> "For My thoughts are not your thoughts,
> Nor are your ways My ways," declares the Lord.
> "For as the heavens are higher than the earth,
> So are My ways higher than your ways
> And My thoughts than your thoughts."

In this scripture, God reminds us that His perspective transcends our limited understanding. As smart, wise, or educated as we may be, God's ways and thoughts are bigger and better than ours. He sees things we can't. He's working behind the scenes in ways we don't even realize.

This means we don't have to have it all figured out because God's wisdom far surpasses our own. That's a humbling truth!

If you're like me, you would prefer if God would just give you a road map or detailed directions for your next steps. But that wouldn't teach us what it means to trust God.

It's tempting to lose hope, wrestle with disappointment, or even give up when things don't go the way we want—when the promotion doesn't happen, a relationship ends, or we get sick at the worst possible time. While we may long for clear answers and immediate solutions, God invites us to trust in His perfect timing and sovereign plan.

He wants you to release your anxieties and uncertainties into His capable hands. Rest in the assurance that God is working all things together for your good.

PRAYER FOR YOUR DAY

God, I'm sorry I lose trust in You when my plans get disrupted. Remind me that Your ways and Your thoughts are higher than mine. Remind me that You know not only the past and the present but also the future. Allow these truths to be embedded in my heart and my mind. In Jesus' name, amen.

> **GOD'S WAYS AND THOUGHTS ARE HIGHER THAN YOURS.**

DAY 84

GROW

Part of building our faith muscles is learning how to trust that God always has a purpose at work—yes, even if the perfectly curated schedule we planned out, the dream we spent years investing in, or the goal we were on the verge of crushing doesn't pan out. These mystery moments are opportunities to exercise our spiritual fitness. As with our physical muscles, much of our spiritual growth happens in periods of stress and tension.

Here are two practical ways to increase your spiritual fitness as you walk through uncertainty.

- **Fuel up on God's promises.** While there are many ways to connect with God, what really strengthens our faith is to read, memorize, and emphasize what God says in His Word. As believers, we need to start believing the promises He gives us in the Bible. That is what this devotional is all about! Don't just gloss over His Word; let it sink in. Pray on it. Post scripture in places you'll see every day. Recite it out loud.
- **Get coached.** It's also important to seek wise counsel. Surrounding ourselves with mentors and friends who share our values and who've walked the path before us is like having the best personal trainers for our spiritual journey. They can spot us when we're struggling, cheer us on, and give us those insights we might not see on our own.

Remember that building our faith muscles isn't a solo adventure; it's a journey best shared with wise guides and nourished by the promises God has laid out for us. Dive deep into those comforting and empowering words, and don't hesitate to lean on the wisdom of those who have been in your shoes. By filling up on God's promises and seeking counsel that steers us right, we're setting ourselves up for a stronger, more resilient faith!

PRAYER FOR YOUR DAY

God, thank You that when life gets hard or uncertain, I can look at it as an opportunity to build spiritual muscle. Remind me of this so I can learn from You rather than wallow in self-pity or shrink in doubt. In Jesus' name, amen.

> **GOD'S WAYS AND THOUGHTS ARE HIGHER THAN YOURS.**

DAY 85

FLOURISH

Today let's read, meditate on, and memorize Isaiah 55:8–9.

I'd like to introduce you to a spiritual discipline called *lectio divina*. This ancient practice helps cultivate a deeper connection with God based on Scripture. It's simple to do and involves four steps:

1. Read the scripture out loud, slowly. Take your time with each word.
2. Reflect on the passage, and consider its meaning and why it matters to you.
3. Respond to God by prayer.
4. Rest in God's presence by contemplating the scripture in silence.

Lectio divina allows you to experience God's presence through His Word and deep contemplation. You can use this practice with any verse or passage in the Bible.

As you meditate on Isaiah 55:8–9, receive the truth that God's ways are perfect, His wisdom is unfathomable, and His love is unending.

PRAYER FOR YOUR DAY

Father, as I think about Your ways and Your works, I'm in awe. It's a humble reminder that You are above all things. Continue to help me surrender my plans for Your better ones. In Jesus' name, amen.

GOD'S WAYS AND THOUGHTS ARE HIGHER THAN YOURS.

WEEK NO. 18

Promise for Your Week:

GOD IS FOREVER FAITHFUL.

Give thanks to the Lord, for He is good,
For His faithfulness is everlasting.

PSALM 136:1

DAY 86

PLOT

You've probably never heard of the sardine run. It's not as famous or well-known as community mud runs or fun runs. The sardine run has everything to do with—you guessed it—sardines!

Imagine millions of these tiny silver fish traveling together in a massive, shimmering wave along the KwaZulu-Natal coastline in South Africa. Dubbed the "Greatest Shoal on Earth," it's like a scene straight out of a nature documentary![26] Every year, usually around May to July, these little fish embark on a journey that's not only a breathtaking spectacle but also a powerful reminder of God's faithfulness. As the sardines migrate, they attract a diverse array of marine life, creating a bustling underwater party. Dolphins, sharks, and birds like gannets all join in, feasting on the abundance of sardines. It wouldn't be surprising to see superpods of dolphins gorging on the sardines while being chased by killer whales. It's a remarkable display of how God provides for His creation, ensuring that every creature has what it needs.

But there's more to the sardine run than just the spectacle. The sardine migration is a perfect example of how God's timing and planning are impeccable. The sardines don't just start their journey randomly. They move when the conditions are just right; the water temperature and currents have to align perfectly. This is a beautiful reminder for us that God's timing in our lives is also perfect. Even when we don't understand why things happen when they do, we can trust that God has a plan, just like He does for the sardines.

So, the next time you think about the ocean or see a documentary on marine life, remember the sardine run. It's not just an incredible natural event—it's a vivid picture of God's provision and His perfect timing. You are part of a much larger plan that's both beautiful and perfectly timed.

PRAYER FOR YOUR DAY

Dear Lord, nothing is by accident. You invite me to partner with You in this life. Thank You that You order my steps and that You care for every detail that concerns me. You are so faithful! In Jesus' name, amen.

GOD IS FOREVER FAITHFUL.

DAY 87

DIG

For most of us, it's much more natural to worry than to give thanks. Today let's shift our focus toward recognizing God's faithfulness.

- Begin with a prayer, inviting the Holy Spirit to guide this time.
- Read Psalm 136 aloud, focusing on the recurring phrase "For His faithfulness is everlasting."
- After reading, take a few moments of silence to let the words sink in. Use an app, a notebook, or a journal to reflect on specific instances in your life where you have experienced God's faithfulness. Think about moments of provision, answered prayers, guidance, protection, or any situation where you felt God's presence.
- Write down at least three specific examples. Include details about how you felt, what happened, and how you saw God's faithfulness in those situations.
- End with a closing prayer.

Take a picture of what you wrote down and keep it with you for the rest of the week. Whenever you catch yourself fraught with anxiety, look at it and be reminded of God's presence and faithfulness in your life. He will never let you down!

A PRAYER FOR YOU FROM ME

Lord God, You are perfectly faithful in everything You do. You show Your faithfulness by caring for, protecting, and providing for us. Forgive our doubts and complaints. Help this reader to trust You fully, even when she is unsure. Guide her to encourage others with Your faithfulness. In Jesus' name, amen.

GOD IS FOREVER FAITHFUL.

DAY 88

PLANT

Psalm 136 is an amazing hymn of praise that highlights God's goodness throughout history. Known as the "Great Hallel" by the Jewish community, it is traditionally sung at the end of the Passover meal. It's likely that Jesus Himself prayed this psalm with His disciples at the Last Supper. The Gospels mention that after singing a hymn, which probably refers to this very psalm (Matthew 26:30 and Mark 14:26), they went to the Mount of Olives.

The whole psalm reads like a beautiful litany. It repeats a certain line twenty-six times: "For His [God's] faithfulness is everlasting." There are certainly times when repetition can be annoying. But in Scripture, repetition is meant to draw us in. This repetition underscores God's amazing works and His ongoing help for His people. In other words, God's faithfulness is limitless. That truth is worth repeating! Some translations substitute the words "mercy" and "loving-kindness" in place of "faithfulness," but all those terms point to one thing: God's character. His goodness remains the same, always and forever.

Consider the ancient nation of Israel. Despite all their mess-ups and wanderings offtrack, God was always there, chasing after them with love and grace. It's an epic love story of God's relentless pursuit of Israel. Even when they messed up and turned their backs on Him to serve other gods time after time after time, He never gave up on them. This serves as a reminder that no matter where we are in life, God is forever faithful.

God has proven Himself to me over and over. I'm grateful for the doors He has opened—and the ones He has closed. Whenever I get anxious, I remind myself that His character is unchanging. I can trust in Him, even if my feelings or plans get rattled.

The promise in Psalm 136:1 holds true every single day.

PRAYER FOR YOUR DAY

Lord, while I long to be free of my trials, I trust in Your perfect wisdom. Thank You for using these challenges as opportunities for love, compassion, and drawing me closer to You. Help me to courageously accept and engage with Your wonderful plans for me. In Jesus' name, amen.

GOD IS FOREVER FAITHFUL.

DAY 89

GROW

In a world where social media trends sweep us off our feet and opinions reign over truth, we can be at peace knowing Jesus offers unwavering faithfulness. I'm reminded of the story of Peter walking on water in Matthew 14. Right after the miraculous feeding of five thousand men (counting women and children, the number was likely closer to ten thousand), Jesus told the disciples to get in a boat and sail to the other side of a lake.

Let's explore three powerful actions Jesus took that reveal His unwavering character and showcase His faithfulness.

- **Jesus sends.** Matthew 14:22 tells us that He "made" the disciples get in the boat (NIV). This makes me think they probably didn't want to go and would much rather have stayed with the multitudes as they celebrated the latest miracle Jesus had performed. But Jesus knows our hearts, our motives, and what the future holds. He knows what we don't know—and that's a lot! He knew the disciples were better off in the boat, even in a storm.
- **Jesus cares.** When the disciples were in the boat, Jesus was on the mountain praying. He wasn't being fawned over by random villagers, nor was He taking a nap. He was seeking wisdom and strength from His Father in heaven. The Bible tells us that when the storm erupted and the disciples started freaking out as they battled the elements, Jesus saw them "straining at the oars—for

the wind was against them—at about the fourth watch of the night, He came to them, walking on the sea; and He intended to pass by them" (Mark 6:48). Jesus sent the men into a storm and paid attention to their struggle. He noticed them. He saw them.
- **Jesus shows up.** Jesus didn't only observe the storm from a distance; He acted. He came to them on the water! "Take courage," He told the disciples. "It is I; do not be afraid" (Matthew 14:27). Jesus showed up when they needed Him most.

Life is bound to throw some storms our way, but here's the silver lining: Jesus never abandons us. He might not always calm the storm, but we can count on Him to weather it by our side.

PRAYER FOR YOUR DAY

Lord, You are so good. You are with me on the peaceful shore and in the raging storm. I know You care. You're all I need, and You will always show up for me. In Jesus' name, amen.

GOD IS FOREVER FAITHFUL.

DAY 90

FLOURISH

Today let's read, meditate on, and memorize Psalm 136:1.

As women of faith, we are called not only to receive God's faithfulness in our lives but also to share it with others. In the story of the Samaritan woman at the well (John 4:7–42), after encountering Jesus, the woman immediately went and told others about her experience. Through sharing her faith, many in her community came to believe in Jesus (v. 39).

Sharing our faith also opens the door for others to share their own stories, creating a ripple effect of God's faithfulness throughout the lives of His people. Consider the ways in which He has shown Himself faithful in your life, both big and small. Then ask God to give you opportunities to share your faith with others.

Whether it's through a conversation with a friend or a social media post, make known what God has done in your life. As you step out in faith, trust that God will use your words to encourage and inspire others and reaffirm His faithfulness in your own heart.

PRAYER FOR YOUR DAY

Heavenly Father, make me a vessel of Your love and grace. Help me to point others to You by sharing all You have done. Thank You for being a steady and constant presence in my life. In Jesus' name, amen.

GOD IS FOREVER FAITHFUL.

WEEK NO. 19

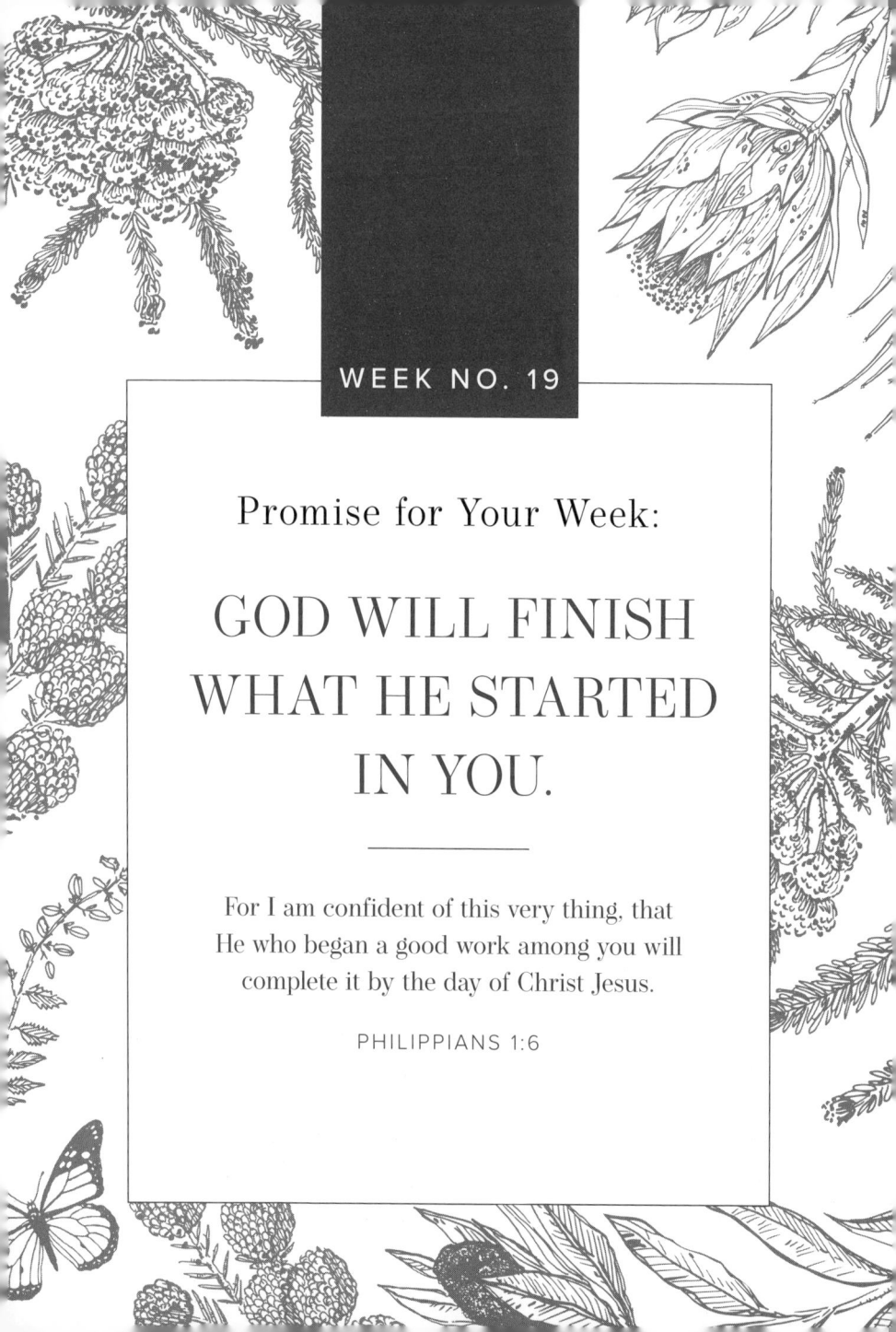

Promise for Your Week:

GOD WILL FINISH WHAT HE STARTED IN YOU.

For I am confident of this very thing, that He who began a good work among you will complete it by the day of Christ Jesus.

PHILIPPIANS 1:6

DAY 91

PLOT

In our fast-paced world, where instant gratification is the norm and success is often measured by immediate results, it's easy to fall into the trap of valuing *performance* over *process*. However, I've learned that God's way of working is quite different. He operates on a divine timeline, patiently and lovingly guiding us to become more like Him—not just in one moment, but *over time*.

In his letter to the Philippians, Paul wrote, "For I am confident of this very thing, that He who began a good work among you will complete it by the day of Christ Jesus" (Philippians 1:6). Paul's words encourage believers that God is not only the initiator of the work in our lives but also the faithful finisher of it. God doesn't abandon us or say, "Good luck. You're on your own now," after our salvation. This encouraging truth means that our journey with God is not about our performance but about learning to fall in love with God's process and trusting His sanctification in our lives.

After my year as Miss Universe, I felt stuck, frustrated, and a little hopeless. It felt like I was making no significant progress in any area of my life. I was so fixated on what to do next, that I never considered what God wanted to teach me in that season. To avoid the "Demi, what's next?" question, I created a second email account, pretended to be my own assistant, and respectfully declined any podcast, interview, or event requests. I had no idea what to tell people, and if I admitted the truth ("Uh, I'm not sure"), I was afraid I'd come off like a giant disappointment.

In that season I got caught up in my own performance, and I attributed my value to knowing my future. I felt like a failure because I didn't know what was next. The truth was, I wasn't a failure in God's eyes. Had I understood the promise of Philippians 1:6, I would have more confidently accepted the new season I was stepping into and not have let that looming question affect my identity.

So, my dear sister, where have you been wrestling with performance? Where do you need to have more grace and embrace God's process in your life? Today you can have confidence that God's way of working is purposeful *and* loving. Take a deep breath and know: He is committed to molding you into the person He created you to be!

PRAYER FOR YOUR DAY

Heavenly Father, thank You for Your faithfulness and love toward me. Give me the courage to let go of my need for control and to fully surrender to You. May I find peace and joy in knowing that You are leading and shaping me into who I'm becoming. In Jesus' name, amen.

GOD WILL FINISH WHAT HE STARTED IN YOU.

DAY 92

DIG

In his book *Atomic Habits*, James Clear writes, "When you fall in love with the process rather than the product, you don't have to wait to give yourself permission to be happy. You can be satisfied anytime your system is running."[27] Too often we believe that only when we achieve certain milestones or overcome specific struggles (i.e., once I lose this weight or get that corner office) can we truly love ourselves or feel valuable. However, this mindset typically leads to disappointment and shame when we inevitably stumble or fall short of our expectations.

Instead, if we shift our focus to embracing the journey of growth, we can find joy and satisfaction in the daily process of becoming more like Christ. Today I want to create space for you to reflect on how God has been working in your life, what He's already brought you through, and where He still wants to shape and sharpen you.

What specific area(s) of your life has God highlighted that needs change? What specific change(s) do you feel God is wanting you to make?

_____

_____

_____

_____

_____

Think and write about specific moments where you've seen God's grace on display. Thank Him for those precious moments.

_____

_____

_____

_____

_____

A PRAYER FOR YOU FROM ME

God, thank You for this special reader. She is infinitely valuable to You! May she delight in Your continuous work in her life, and may Your grace empower her to walk in obedience. In Jesus' name, amen.

GOD WILL FINISH WHAT HE STARTED IN YOU.

DAY 93

PLANT

Psalm 66:1–3 kicks off with a big, joyful invitation to praise God with all our hearts:

> Shout joyfully to God, all the earth;
> Sing the glory of His name;
> Make His praise glorious.
> Say to God, "How awesome are Your works!"

These three verses should make you do a little dance in the morning when you get out of bed! The tone is clearly one of excitement and awe, celebrating God's greatness. But then, a few verses later, the passage takes a surprising turn:

> For You have put us to the test, God;
> You have refined us as silver is refined.
> You brought us into the net;
> You laid an oppressive burden upon us.
> You made men ride over our heads;
> We went through fire and through water.
> Yet You brought us out into a place of abundance.
> (vv. 10–12)

Talk about an instant mood change. The psalmist went from jumping up and down to having a crushing weight on his back! At first this abrupt shift may seem odd or even contradictory. But as we take a closer look, we see that these two sections of the psalm are actually intertwined.

The praise in verses 1–3 is not disconnected from the trials described in verses 10–12; rather, it is precisely because of God's faithfulness and deliverance in the midst of adversity that the psalmist can offer such praise. Just as silver is refined in the furnace, so, too, are God's people refined through trials and hardships. Of course these experiences don't feel good in the moment, but they ultimately serve to purify and strengthen our faith. As the psalmist declared, God brought Israel through fire and water to "a place of abundance."

Remember that your struggles are not in vain; they are part of God's continuous work in your life. Strive to find joy in the process, knowing that God's hand is guiding you, refining you, and leading you to a place of abundance.

PRAYER FOR YOUR DAY

Father, thank You that I get to trust Your faithfulness in the midst of my challenges. Strengthen me with resilience as I journey toward the place of abundance that You have prepared for me. In Jesus' name, amen.

GOD WILL FINISH WHAT HE STARTED IN YOU.

DAY 94

GROW

We've learned that we can have confidence that our God finishes what He starts. He always keeps His word and accomplishes what He sets out to do.

God promised Noah that He would save his family from the flood—and He did. God promised Abraham and Sarah that they would have a son at a very old age—and they did. God promised to rescue the Israelites out of Egyptian slavery and bring them to a special land flowing with milk and honey—and He did. God promised to bring exile and destruction to Israel because of their disobedience—and He did. God always completes His task.

Even Jesus, while experiencing the excruciating pain of crucifixion, breathed His last breath and cried out, "It is finished!" (John 19:30). In one simple phrase, Jesus communicated the completion of God's plan for the payment of our sin. You see, all throughout Scripture, God's résumé speaks for itself: *He finishes what He starts.*

David understood this very well when he wrote, "The LORD will accomplish what concerns me" (Psalm 138:8). Over the last few days, we've talked about focusing on process rather than performance, trusting God's work in our life over time, and how even trials can bring us to a place of abundance. Each of these helps build a stronger framework for truly accepting God's promise in Philippians 1:6.

It's easy to forget how most good things take time to come to fruition—getting a degree, raising a child through adulthood, learning a new language, healing from an injury. Life with Christ is no different. Growing in spiritual maturity does not come at the snap of a finger. It takes time. Just as bread needs time to rise and bake to perfection, our faith requires patience, perseverance, and a willingness to embrace the process. We need to patiently posture ourselves before God and trust that He's bringing us to completion!

Today let's lean into the truth that God is indeed a *finisher*. From the promises fulfilled in Scripture to the ultimate completion of Jesus' work on the cross, God's track record speaks for itself. You and I are His good creation; we can walk with confidence, knowing God wants us to transform into the likeness of Jesus.

PRAYER FOR YOUR DAY

God, thank You for the countless examples of Your faithfulness throughout Scripture. May we find joy in the journey, knowing that You are bringing us to a place of greater maturity and likeness to Your Son. In Jesus' name, amen.

GOD WILL FINISH WHAT HE STARTED IN YOU.

DAY 95

FLOURISH

Today let's read, meditate on, and memorize Philippians 1:6.

How do you see God working in your life right now?

As you move forward in confidence, here are two practical reminders:

Open your hands and receive. We are often our own harshest critic, but God's love for you is unconditional. He delights in your efforts to grow and learn, not because you're perfect but because you are His. He freely gives His grace, so open your hands and receive it. His grace is a gift freely given. So let go of self-judgment, open your hands, and receive it.

Learn instead of ignore. Every situation is a learning opportunity—even sin or setback. Our natural response to shame, which started with Adam and Eve in the garden, is to hide. But rather than ignoring an opportunity for growth, let's embrace it. Each experience, whether positive or negative, has the potential to teach us something valuable about ourselves and about God's character.

PRAYER FOR YOUR DAY

Heavenly Father, You are so good! Thank You for seeing me, hearing me, and working in me. I'm not who I once was, and I'm so excited for who I'm becoming with Christ. Continue to cover me with Your grace as I strive to live a life that gives You glory. In Jesus' name, amen.

GOD WILL FINISH WHAT HE STARTED IN YOU.

WEEK NO. 20

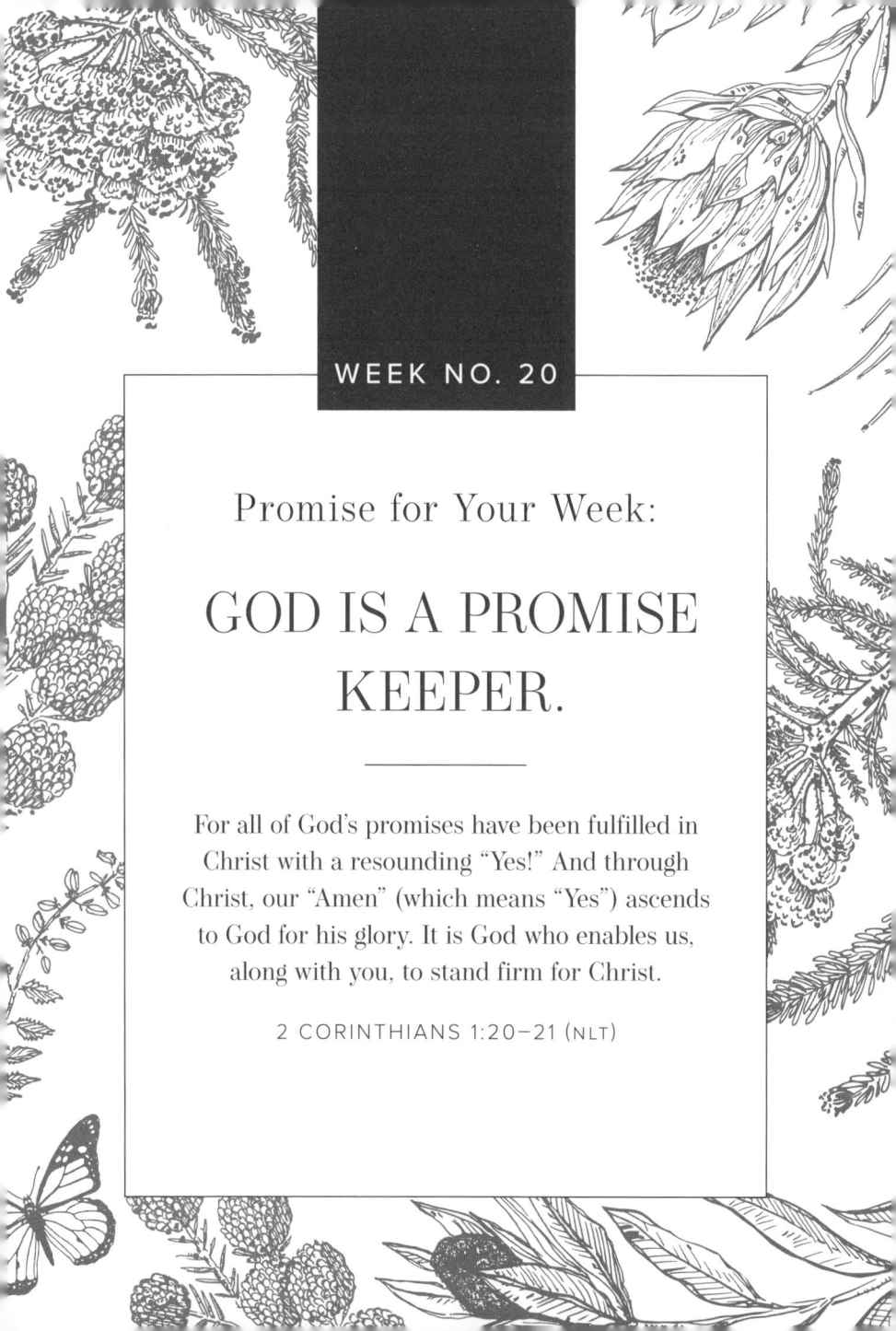

Promise for Your Week:

GOD IS A PROMISE KEEPER.

For all of God's promises have been fulfilled in Christ with a resounding "Yes!" And through Christ, our "Amen" (which means "Yes") ascends to God for his glory. It is God who enables us, along with you, to stand firm for Christ.

2 CORINTHIANS 1:20–21 (NLT)

DAY 96

PLOT

I've learned over the years that many of my struggles have started with the same word: *self*. *Self*-love, *self*-worth, and even *self*-confidence. That insecurity might come as a surprise since I've had opportunities to speak in front of large audiences, traveled the world in the public eye, and carried a title like Miss Universe. But I'm still a girl who has dealt with hurt, fear of failure, and the many valleys that come with the roller coaster of life. And so, I've struggled with my confidence. Can you relate?

The definition of *confidence* translates to having "full trust." Therefore, self-confidence would mean that we have full trust in ourselves. Now, after having spent nineteen weeks together, you've probably learned that I have failed many times when I've tried to rely on . . . *myself*. When we trust in ourselves, we will inevitably fall short. Eventually, we will realize that our self-confidence is temporary and runs dry at some point.

But I have great news! We don't have to make it through the day alone, and we don't have to rely on ourselves. We can rely on something—*Someone*—much more trustworthy: God. God-confidence is full trust in *Him*, not in ourselves. It's a full confidence that His love for us is everlasting and unchanging.

Perhaps you're thinking, *Have God-confidence! That sounds easy enough. It's catchy too!* But it's not so simple to shift from self-confidence to God-confidence. This week I look forward to exploring a question

I have studied long and hard: Why do we get to have confidence in God?

Throughout this devotional, we have studied nineteen promises from God. I have reserved this last week of our journey to unbreakable faith for the one promise that, in my opinion, sums up all nineteen promises we have worked through so far. The Bible is full of promises from God—not just promises rooted in hope, but in hope with assurance. You see, our God is not just a promise *maker*, He's a promise *keeper*.

My friend Lysa TerKeurst told me that trust is built not just with time but with time plus believable behavior. So when we consider how God has behaved toward us (and His people) in the past, can we trust Him? If we can't trust God, then how can we do life with Him? And if we can't do life with Him, then what is our reward?

This week we are going to look at God as the ultimate Promise Keeper—to understand that we can have confidence in Him because of who He is and the promises He's kept (2 Corinthians 1:20–21).

PRAYER FOR YOUR DAY

Dear Jesus, thank You for Your continued faithfulness in my life. When I am faced with doubt, remind me of the truth rooted in Your promises. Thank You for always being trustworthy. In Jesus' name, amen.

GOD IS A PROMISE KEEPER.

DAY 97

DIG

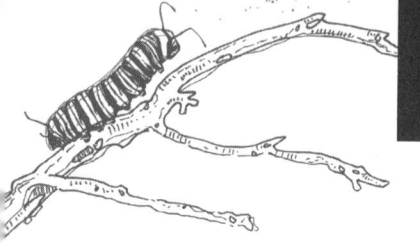

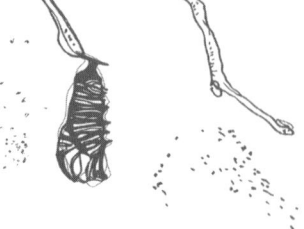

Yesterday we addressed how self-confidence falls short. But you might still be wondering if self-confidence is really such a bad thing. Perhaps you believe that it can lead to good things, like taking risks, meeting new people, and having greater academic performance. Of course it can! Confidence can have lots of benefits, especially when it highlights your capabilities and competencies. When you know and show your strengths, it becomes easier to trust yourself.

However, if I put full trust in myself, bad things can happen very quickly, especially if I'm unequipped for a situation. Complete trust in myself leads to stubbornness, underestimating challenges, and an unwillingness to seek wise counsel. And then when failure inevitably occurs, insecurity quickly creeps in.

Trusting yourself has its benefits and value, but relying on self-confidence alone is unreliable because our capabilities are limited. Trusting in myself alone will certainly lead to disappointment sooner rather than later.

Can you recall a time when trusting yourself led to something beneficial?

_____

_____

_____

_____

Can you recall a time when having self-confidence didn't lead to a good result?

_____

_____

_____

What do you think are the differences between these two types of experiences?

_____

_____

_____

A PRAYER FOR YOU FROM ME

Dear heavenly Father, I ask that You remove the pressure from this daughter of Yours to rely on her own capabilities. Please fill her with the confidence that can come only from trusting in You and relying on Your unlimited power. In Jesus' name, amen.

GOD IS A PROMISE KEEPER.

DAY 98

PLANT

One of the greatest developments in ancient warfare was the chariot, which gave the upper hand to any army. In fact, kings were so proud of their chariots that they would often brag about how many they had. Even King Solomon gloated about his chariots (1 Kings 4:26).

Psalm 20:7 confirms how beloved chariots were, but how the people of God had a different source of trust: "Some trust in chariots and some in horses, but we trust in the name of the LORD our God" (NIV). Unlike the ancient kings, who trusted in what could get them through a temporary battle, we can trust in God's character, something far more lasting. We know that God is a creator, provider, savior, friend, and good Father. Let's take a few moments to look over some verses that affirm these truths.

Characteristics	Scripture
God is a creator.	But now, thus says the LORD, your Creator, O Jacob, and He who formed you, O Israel, "Do not fear, for I have redeemed you; I have called you by name; you are Mine!" (Isaiah 43:1 NASB1995)
God is a provider.	Jesus then said to them, "Truly, truly, I say to you, it is not Moses who has given you the bread out of heaven, but it is My Father who gives you the true bread out of heaven."(John 6:32 NASB1995)

Characteristics	Scripture
God is a good Father.	So that He might redeem those who were under the Law, that we might receive the adoption as sons. Because you are sons, God has sent forth the Spirit of His Son into our hearts, crying, "Abba! Father!" (Galatians 4:5–6 NASB1995)
God is a savior.	But when the kindness of God our Savior and His love for mankind appeared, He saved us, not on the basis of deeds which we have done in righteousness, but according to His mercy, by the washing of regeneration and renewing by the Holy Spirit. (Titus 3:4–5 NASB1995)
God is a friend.	And the Scripture was fulfilled which says, "And Abraham believed God, and it was reckoned to him as righteousness," and he was called the friend of God. (James 2:23 NASB1995)

Our God is an all-powerful creator and provider, but He is also our good Father who chooses to save us and treat us like a friend. Because of God's trustworthy character throughout eternity, we can put our full trust in Him!

PRAYER FOR YOUR DAY

Lord, show me more and more of Your character every day. Teach me Your ways and lead me down Your paths. Help me to understand You better in Your vast complexity and to trust Your love for me. In Jesus' name, amen.

GOD IS A PROMISE KEEPER.

DAY 99

GROW

Even if I know God's character well, it can still be difficult to trust Him fully, especially when my emotions get the best of me. When my sister was diagnosed with brain dysgenesis, there were years when I was angry about her diagnosis and struggled to trust the plan and purpose God had for her life. In those moments, I had to remind myself that when my emotions are fickle, God is steadfast.

God shows His steadfast character throughout the Old Testament. In one example, King David, the first faithful king of Israel, asked God if he could build Him a temple, but God rejected his offer, saying that David's son Solomon would build the temple instead. God then promised David in 2 Samuel 7:12–16 that his lineage would be established for generations to come. Even though it didn't happen the way David asked, God made a promise—one that He would keep.

Many years later, the kings of Israel started to forget God's grace and love. At least five times in 1 and 2 Kings, God showed mercy to the nation of Israel and its kings even though they acted wickedly. God's reason for showing them this kindness was to uphold His promise to David, which He had made decades prior (1 Kings 11:12; 15:4; 2 Kings 8:19; 19:34; 20:6).

This is a beautiful reminder that God is faithful to keep His promises despite how much we mess up. God is worthy of our full trust. And the greatest promise that He offers you and me is that when He looks at us, He sees Jesus, just like He saw David in place of those kings. Because of Jesus' life, death, and resurrection, we can be forgiven for all our shortcomings and live with His Spirit here on earth, as well as face-to-face with Him forever.

In the NIV translation of Psalm 20, the word "victory" is mentioned three times as a testament that those who hold on to God-confidence will eventually have victory because of Jesus' sacrifice and resurrection. This confidence in our victory because of Christ allows us to live dependent on the Lord even when our emotions are fickle.

PRAYER FOR YOUR DAY

Lord, be with me today. Remind me of Your great works and consistency in my life. Give me hope for the future and help me trust You more every day. I love You, Lord. I want to experience Your victory in my life. In Jesus' name, amen.

> **GOD IS A PROMISE KEEPER.**

DAY 100

FLOURISH

Today let's read, meditate on, and memorize 2 Corinthians 1:20–21. If I can't rely on *self*-confidence because I am a fallible human, then that rules out *others*-confidence as well. Everyone is just as fickle and unpredictable as me! *God*-confidence, however, looks to the trustworthy Creator of the universe who loves each of us dearly.

If God truly honors His promises, as Paul reminded us, why wouldn't we offer Him our complete trust? Embracing full God-confidence requires letting go of self-reliance, as Jesus invites us to pick up our cross—our means of surrender—and follow Him.

We may chase dreams like financial freedom and fulfilling relationships, but these can never replace God. We must release our grip on what we love and open our hands to our loving Father, saying, "Don't give me what I'm chasing, Father; give me what You're pursuing." This is God-confidence—full trust in a loving, promise-keeping God. It's a complete surrender to hold tightly to our Father, which naturally cultivates an unbreakable faith.

PRAYER FOR YOUR DAY

Lord, help me build my trust in You daily so that I can commit myself to You like You are committed to Your promises. Help me release my own will and chase what You desire. I love You, Lord. Amen.

GOD IS A PROMISE KEEPER.

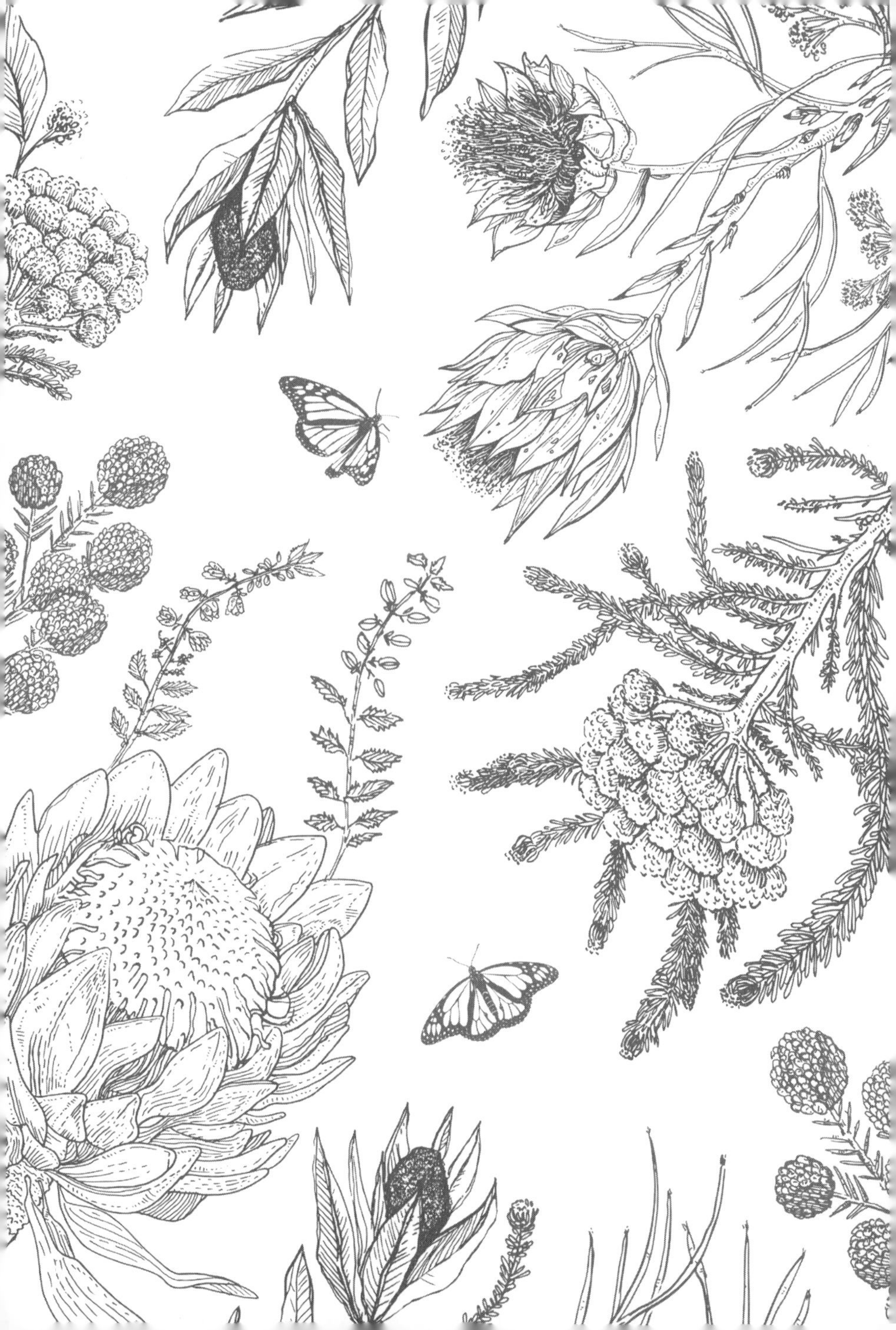

FINAL THOUGHTS

Thank you for spending the last hundred days with me. Even though I wrote this devotional with you on my heart, completing it felt like giving myself a little gift by eliminating false beliefs in my own life. I hope that these last hundred days reminded you that God sees you as worthy, forgiven, precious, worth it, shame-free, a co-laborer with Him, a daughter of the one true King, and royalty waiting to be welcomed home.

My prayer is that these twenty truths will produce a confidence in you that doesn't come from the superficial assurances we find on trendy social media pages, from our most encouraging friends, or even from our biggest accomplishments, but rather from promises rooted in our never-changing, always trustworthy, and faithful God.

In moments when the Enemy urges you to doubt or question who you are, turn to the biblical truths you have memorized here. They are a proven solid ground that have stood the test of time—just like God's love for you.

ACKNOWLEDGMENTS

A J Gregory, your guidance and input were invaluable. Thank you for your insightful feedback, professionalism, and unwavering support. What a joy to work with you!

Wyatt Edwards and Wesley Newman, I am so grateful for your dedication as my research consultants and support team. Your attention to detail and commitment to each devotional entry did not go unnoticed. Thank you for your incredible effort and teamwork!

My whole Thomas Nelson team: Stephanie Newton, vice president and publisher; Kara Mannix, acquisitions editor; Bonnie Honeycutt, senior editor; Lydia Eagle, marketing director; Tiffany Forrester, art director. I am deeply thankful to my amazing book team for their unwavering dedication, expertise, and passion in bringing this project to fruition.

The Tebow Group, thank you for always striving for excellence, for being true team players, and for always supporting me in every project we get to work on together. You truly bring your best; it's so fun to do life with you guys!

NOTES

1. Jennifer Guttman, "The Relationship with Yourself," *Psychology Today*, June 27, 2019, https://www.psychologytoday.com/us/blog/sustainable-life-satisfaction/201906/the-relationship-yourself.
2. Kara Powell and Brad M. Griffin, *3 Big Questions That Change Every Teenager: Making the Most of Your Conversations and Connections* (Baker, 2021).
3. Timothy Keller and Kathy Keller, *The Meaning of Marriage: Facing the Complexities of Commitment with the Wisdom of God* (Riverhead Books, 2013), 101.
4. W. Günther and C. Brown, "Φιλέω," ed. Lothar Coenen, Erich Beyreuther, and Hans Bietenhard, *New International Dictionary of New Testament Theology* (Zondervan, 1986), 4: 548.
5. Willem VanGemeren, ed., *New International Dictionary of Old Testament Theology & Exegesis* (Zondervan, 1997), 4: 251.
6. Willem VanGemeren, ed., *New International Dictionary of Old Testament Theology & Exegesis* (Zondervan, 1997), 4: 615.
7. Matthew 9:1–8; Mark 2:1–12; Luke 5:17–26.
8. Daniel Isaac Block, *Judges, Ruth: An Exegetical and Theological Exposition of Holy Scripture*, The New American Commentary (Broadman & Holman, 1999), 6: 652.
9. Dictionary.com, s.v. "shame," accessed November 21, 2024, https://www.dictionary.com/browse/shame.
10. Brené Brown, "Shame vs. Guilt," Brené Brown, January 15, 2013, https://brenebrown.com/articles/2013/01/15/shame-v-guilt/.
11. Epictetus, *Discourses* 3.22.52, (William Heinemann, 1969).

12. H. G. Liddell, *A Lexicon: Abridged from Liddell and Scott's Greek-English Lexicon* (Logos Research Systems, 1996), 651.
13. Pierrette Mimi Poinsett, ed., "Cerebral Dysgenesis and Cerebral Palsy," Cerebral Palsy Guidance, updated December 17, 2024, https://www.cerebralpalsyguidance.com/cerebral-palsy/causes/cerebral-dysgenesis/.
14. Olivia Guy-Evans, "Cerebellum: Functions, Structure, and Location," *Simple Psychology*, updated September 18, 2023, https://www.simplypsychology.org/what-is-the-cerebellum.html.
15. Matthew Henry, John 3 Bible Commentary, Christianity.com, accessed November 22, 2024, https://www.christianity.com/bible/commentary/matthew-henry-complete/john/3.
16. "Trust," The High Calling by Theology of Work, September 29, 2002, https://www.theologyofwork.org/the-high-calling/audio/trust/.
17. I recommend Biblehub.com or their app, EnduringWord.com, the ESV Bible app, and Logos Bible software.
18. "Crime Stats: Compare Key Data on South Africa & United States," NationMaster, accessed November 22, 2024, https://www.nationmaster.com/country-info/compare/South-Africa/United-States/Crime.
19. Daryl Austin, "More Americans Than Ever Are Afraid of the Dark, Experts Say. Here's Why," *USA Today*, June 2, 2023, https://www.usatoday.com/story/life/health-wellness/2022/03/01/are-you-afraid-dark-why-pandemic/6782349001/.
20. Austin, "More Americans Than Ever Are Afraid of the Dark."
21. Leviticus 1:1; Deuteronomy 33:4.
22. William Barclay, *Educational Ideals in the Ancient World* (Baker, 1974), 11–13.
23. Matthew 4:1–10.
24. "Sword Drill," Pure Desire Ministries, accessed November 22, 2024, https://puredesire.org/wp-content/uploads/2020/12/sword-drill-3.pdf.
25. Bruce K. Waltke and Fred G. Zaspel, *How to Read and Understand the Psalms* (Crossway, 2023), 12.

26. "Sardine Run," Wild Safari Guide, accessed November 23, 2024, https://wildsafariguide.com/experiences/natural-phenomena/sardine-run/.
27. James Clear, *Atomic Habits: An Easy & Proven Way to Build Good Habits & Break Bad Ones* (Penguin Random House, 2018), 26.

ABOUT THE AUTHOR

Demi-Leigh Tebow is an entrepreneur, speaker, and bestselling author who finds great joy and purpose in encouraging and inspiring other women. She was crowned Miss South Africa and Miss Universe in 2017 and speaks regularly around the globe. She is the bestselling author of *A Crown That Lasts* and her first children's book, *Princess Paris Finds Her Purpose*.

Demi strives to bring compassion to people who are hurting as well as being a voice for the unheard victims of human trafficking all over the world. She also desires to use her entrepreneurial gift and social media presence as platforms for meaningful cultural change. Demi hopes to be a light for others by sharing her own stories of healing and freedom, guiding women to find their power in Christ and to overcome obstacles. After surviving a horrific attempted carjacking in South Africa, Demi started the Unbreakable campaign, which aims to educate and uplift women, teaching them to find strength within. Demi is also the big sister of Franje Peters, who was born with cerebellar agenesis and passed away on May 4, 2019. Through her unique relationship with her sister, Demi has developed a strong passion for supporting people with special needs and disabilities.

When she's not traveling the world and sharing hope with others, Demi resides in the United States with her husband, Tim Tebow, and her three fur babies: Chunk, Paris, and Kobe (aka "The Tebow Pack").